malcolm gluck's
brave new world

malcolm gluck's
brave new world

Why the wines of Australia, California, New Zealand, and South Africa taste the way they do

With photographs by the author

MITCHELL BEAZLEY

To Robert Freson, *photographe extraordinaire*, who never guessed how much he passed on.

Brave New World
First published in Great Britain in 2006 by Mitchell Beazley
an imprint of Octopus Publishing Group Ltd,
2–4 Heron Quays, London E14 4JP

ISBN 13: 978 1 84533 185 6
ISBN 10: 1 84533 185 0
A CIP catalogue copy of this book is available
from the British Library

Commissioning Editor: Hilary Lumsden
Executive Art Editor: Nicky Collings, Yasia Williams
Design: John Round Design
Senior Editor: Julie Sheppard
Editor: Susan Keevil
Editorial Assistant: Philippa Bell
Proofreader: Samantha Stokes
Indexer: John Noble
Production: Faizah Malik

Printed and bound in China by Toppan Printing Company

TITLE PAGE Hamiliton-Russell produces not just one of South Africa's most complete Pinot Noirs but, on occasions, one of the planet's most limpid expressions of this grape.

Contents

Introduction
Colourless green ideas sleep furiously

"The trouble with people is not that they don't know
but that they know so much that ain't so."

Henry Wheeler Shaw, Josh Billings' *Encyclopedia of Wit and Wisdom*.

This is a book about people as much as it is about wine and the places, often exquisitely photogenic, where it is made. For what do we hold in our hands when we contemplate a glass of wine? We hold a history to be sure (of wine itself, stretching back more than seven thousand years). We hold a particular liquid (with its own history of regionality and provenance, its own spirit of place). We hold, though, something more immediately sensational: a human artefact which only a human being can appreciate and only another human being can have made.

For wine is made. Make no mistake about it. It cannot simply be grown, no more than letters and words can rearrange themselves without effort and create coherent sentences, thoughts, declarations (of love or war). May I invite you to consider wine like this? Just as letters require human intervention to be sorted out and made meaningfully into words and sentences so do grapes need to be sorted and pressed to become a mouth-watering alcoholic drink. Wine is an expression of locality, yes, but that locality, that expression, is, to my mind, less about local soil and more about local soul.

Wines begin as vines being grown in vineyards, so their successful upbringing hangs upon viticulture, but their transformation into wine depends on interpretation by the winemaker(s). It follows from this that the glass of wine in our hands, whatever its grape and vineyard, would be a different wine if someone else had made it from those same grapes, from the same vineyard. As David Darlington observed in his book, *Angel's Visits – An Enquiry into the Mystery of Zinfandel* (Henry Holt & Co, New York 1991): "...after David Bennion relinquished the Ridge winemaking to Paul Draper, Ridge wines became less and less like Dave Bennion and more and more like Paul Draper." Each and every wine, however noble, however vastly overpriced, however humble or rustic, is an expression of those human endeavours called winemaking and grape growing. But there are those who insist on that mystical something called terroir. It is perhaps the most frequently used, and abused, term in the rich vein of language (obfuscation, hollow jargon, winespeak) mined by the traditionalist, hyperbolic wine writer, the wine producer,

and the wine merchant and, sadly, ritually swallowed by wine collectors and snobby wine drinkers: those individuals who consume labels rather than critically relishing liquids, obeying the edicts of the price-fixers rather than considering the evidence of their own senses (and who may, in truth, be unable to tell a cheap Grenache from a toweringly expensive Merlot, yet choose the latter for no other reason than that it is expensive and, to the superficial judge at least, prestigious). Yet the biggest elements of terroir are overwhelmingly human and therefore it is as irrational to worship a vineyard for its self-proclaimed enduring excellence, as hallowed vines, as it is to believe that a house which is a delight to visit when the grand Bosendorfer family inhabits it will offer the same rich welcome and exude the same sweet charm when it is sold and the upright Underwoods live there. No estate agent would dare promote the sale of property on such specious grounds, yet thousands of wine magnates, thousands of wine merchants, and scores of wine writers promulgate similar mendacious myths about the wines they produce, sell, and write about. Terroir is a green idea sleeping furiously.[1]

Gullible fools lap up this nonsense because they are dazzled by romantic notions, a horizon encircled with myths,[2] instead of the evidence of what is under their noses. What else is required to make a

PREVIOUS PAGE The raw material of wine is the highly manipulated fruit of a complex plant. Further human intervention during all stages of winemaking adds more complexities which are always the determinants of the wine's style.

BELOW Moonshine into wine. The earth's satellite comes up over Goldwater Estate's new vineyard planting, on Waiheke Island, New Zealand.

RIGHT Company car at Woodstock Winery, McLaren Vale, South Australia. Transports of delight are not only provided by the local Shiraz and Chardonnay.

judgement about a wine than that it is tasted? Or would you wed
someone chosen from the equivalent of a seed catalogue? Buy unseen
a car over the phone? Many wines are tasted blind of course, by
professional wine judges and tasters, and routinely the so-called famed
and great wines, from vineyards considered legendary, are shown to be
second best, often third and fifth best, to wines from vineyards of no
fame whatsoever.

All that is required of a vineyard to grow worthy wine grapes is
that it gets sufficient sun to ripen the bunches, cooler nights to coax
sympathetic acids (so a tropical climate is not ideal), and that it is free-
draining to permit the vines to seek deeper soils rather than superficial
nourishment from shallow-lying water. It may or may not require
irrigation in hot weather. It will certainly demand close attention during
the growing season (from pruning to pest management). Yes, the variety
must suit the soil, situation, and climate and there must be limits set on

---

[1] "Green ideas which sleep furiously", Noam Chomsky, *Syntactic Structures* (1957), providing an
instance of a grammatically perfect sentence which is utterly meaningless.

[2] "Only a horizon encircled with myths can mark off a cultural movement as a discrete unit,"
wrote Nietzsche in *The Birth of Tragedy*, following his disenchantment with Wagner. It is an
insight into any social, political, religious, ideological, or artistic creed based upon faith
without rational proofs. The hi-falutin cultural movement which elevates wine to an artistic,
rather than at best (and then only sometimes) a merely creative endeavour, and which insists
subsoils sculpt wine – a movement to which many winemakers, wine writers, and wine
promotors subscribe – is surrounded by myths as far as the eye can see. It is one of two vinous
effects which can render the imbiber horizontal. I prefer the one which wears off.

THIS PAGE Machinery in the vineyard, technology in the winery, science in the winemaking. None sounds romantic, though the liquid in the glass may be.

RIGHT Exciting food and sensual wines get on very well together at Charles Back's Fairview Estate, Paarl, South Africa.

yields. Vineyards on slopes may be preferable to those on the flat, but even here there is plentiful evidence to suggest this, in many wine areas, is a marginal plus. Organic vineyards grow more sensual fruit than those which receive the odd chemical, but the latter may produce a superior wine because the winemaker is more attentive, more skilled.

All wines have textures: velvety, satin-smooth, or leathery, for example. No wine writer scorns these terms and there are several more. The terroirists, those who insist each vineyard is so individual from another that its characteristics are discernible in the wine, also employ texture, but they have only two to call on, flannel and wool. They employ flannel in order to pull the wool over your eyes.

This book, among other things, sees the winemaker as the most crucial element in the creation of a wine, thus negating the idea that vineyards, though obviously crucial as the raw materials' source, have a magic independent of people. In my view the enshrinement, in French wine laws, of the regulations concerned with *appellation contrôlée* are merely a superb wheeze to protect real estate values and maintain a bureaucratic stranglehold. Can anything, for example, have been more officiously Lewis Carollian than the AOC authorities in 1964 demanding that Château Cheval Blanc, for me an epiphanal St Emilion, plant Cabernet Sauvignon vines as the producer's emphasis on Cabernet Franc and Merlot was irregular?

This book is, mostly, a celebration of individuals (not celebrities) free of such insane restraints. Of course the Old World has individuals also – hundreds of them making wondrous wines – and the New World is not without its wines which elect, like some of the Old World's clothed-yet-naked emperors, to be valued for their scarcity and huge price rather than for the sheer joy of the liquid in the bottles. Personally, I have never felt Australia's

Grange or California's Opus One justified the hype each encouraged.

There is as yet no scientific evidence, geological, chemical, or botanical, to prove that any mineral or soil constituents of any vineyard are so powerful that they can pass into the grapes and be recognized on the nose and palate. True, apples, cherries, mangoes, and many other fruits can vividly display their provenance upon being tasted. But a wine grape is not encountered in the same way. The journey from vineyard to wine glass is so serpentine, so rich in human manipulation, that it is barely recognizable from the berry on the vine.

True, a few large vineyard areas produce wines which have characteristics in common on the nose and palate. But this is because the winemakers in such areas all make their wines the same way from the same single grape variety. The winemakers aim for homogeneity. They want their wines to be identifiably a Moselle Riesling, or a Loire Cabernet Franc, or a Coonawarra Cabernet Sauvignon. The moment one of these winemakers veers from the norm, the wine is no longer one of a kind, but something different. The soil of the vineyard is less important than the soul of the winemaker.

A powerfully distinct subsoil type in a few large denominated areas may, then, pass on something to certain of its wines if winemakers follow the rules. I do not wish to challenge this. What I want to challenge is the absurdity that each individual vineyard, solely because it is this vineyard in this spot and no other, is thereby capable of creating a wholly individual wine that is markedly noticeable under scrutiny, worth a fortune, and that its grape growers and winemakers are mere passive conjurors, puppets manipulated by the vineyard, helpless in the grip of terroir to produce anything other than what the soil dictates. What utter fanciful poppycock. Insanity indeed. ("All power of fancy over reason is a degree of insanity," Dr Johnson, *Rasselas*).

Once one concedes that it is important to maintain scepticism in the face of the pressure to believe the twaddle talked about the Old World's famous vineyard areas and their wines, it becomes possible to accept the notion that New World vineyards are every bit as productively exciting because so many of the people running them want to make thrilling wines.

It is clear, for example, that Pinot Noir from Burgundy is not any more capable because of its soil (and whatever vineyard you care to name) of providing a markedly different, uniquely Burgundian, bouquet and flavour than a Pinot Noir from, say, the Russian River Valley in California or Gippsland in Victoria. I have experienced from both these latter places Pinots of sufficient precision and purpose to knock many a fantastically priced burgundy into a cocked *chapeau*.

What was the deciding factor then? The answer is obvious. It was the winemaker. Not for nothing are so many Sancerrois flocking to Marlborough to see how it is that the Kiwis are producing more biting Sauvignons Blancs than they are. No-one is suggesting that the French buy millions of tons of Marlbrough's soil, ship it back to France, and hey presto! Sancerre's fortunes are restored. Those guys are going out there to see how the people do it. As winemakers change, so will their wines. The answer ain't in the soil. Yes, of course, climate will play a part (and Marlborough's being maritime is clearly more character-building for a Sauvignon Blanc grape than Sancerre's), but the main things any Sancerrois will take back with him/her to the Loire are insight, knowledge, and new skills.

This book is a celebration of these latter virtues as found, to this single taster (and so this is a partial not a complete list of all the most gripping of New World wines), on my travels with tasting glass, pen, and camera. It is a brisk tour to meet some winemakers; a visual and verbal record of a long journey around the world and I would make only one further comment about it: in all of these countries English is the language of winemaking (whatever local or imported tongues may also be spoken). People who speak English as a first, or *primus inter pares*, language are, as a general tendency, like that language itself,

ABOVE The legendary Pinot Noirs of Otago, New Zealand, cannot quite compete for natural beauty with nearby Lake Wakatipu, Queenstown.

RIGHT Father and son, George and Mick Unti, of Unti Vineyards, Healdsburg, California, are partial to Zinfandel, Sangiovese, Syrah, and Barbera from their own vines.

open to ideas, generous to admit neologisms, and sceptical of hard and fast rules. It shows in the wines.

Indeed, *English-Speaking Wines*[3] was, for a while, one of the titles toyed with for this book. It is an apposite title and one which may, to the enquiring mind, also suggest why such wines have so taken the world by storm (if this cliché has not now become dangerously devalued by the various impacts of global warming).

The photographs here are the fruits of some seven or eight years of snapping away. But the ideas, the paragraphs, are the result of over forty years of drinking and thinking about wine and they are not lightly enscribed. They are written on my heart. Somewhat shortened, they can serve on my tombstone.

[3] Not just English-speaking wine, but English-drinking wine. By 2008 it has been estimated that the amount of money the Brits spend on wine will reach a staggering £6 billion. The only country expected to spend more is the USA. The UK will, then, be the biggest wine-drinking market in Europe. In the last four years, as a matter of interest, UK wine sales have rocketed over twenty-one per cent. In 2003 the British got through 1.5 billion bottles of wine. This is expected to increase to 1.74 billion bottles by 2008. This growth in consumption is mirrored by the increase in the popularity of wines made by the English-speaking winemakers of Australia, California, New Zealand, and South Africa. The Old World is being soundly beaten by the New World at its own game (and the rules of that game are having to be written and rewritten to take account of the New World's challenge).

EXPLODING THE MYTH

In March 2005, a most illuminating paper was presented at the Royal Economic Society's annual conference. It was prepared by Olivier Gergaud of the University of Reims and Victor Ginsburgh of the Université Libre de Bruxelles. Their findings were dynamite, utterly exploding the idea of terroir. It was, these two academics said, not terroir which determined the quality of a wine but the "winemaking technologies". The two men collected data on environmental conditions and winemaking techniques in 100 vineyards of the Haut-Médoc in 1990, including the first-growths such as châteaux Mouton-Rothschild, Latour, Lafite-Rothschild, and Margaux. "In the Médoc region the French terroir legend does not hold," they reported. I would confidently assert that if they carried out the same research in the vineyards of Burgundy, the Rhône, Loire, and anywhere else in France, let alone the world, the results, *mutatis mutandis*, would be the same. It is not terroir which makes a wine, it is human intervention. Of course, the old-school wine merchants in cahoots with (and dependent upon) French wine producers will have it differently. Terroir is everything, they'll tell you, but these people have to peddle terroir because the wines they deal in demand it. Of course they will. The conclusion reached by the two academics cited here begs a fundamental question: in whose interest is it to promulgate and nourish the notion of terroir when it flies in the face of rationality? The answer is, it seems to me, twofold: firstly, it has an attractive "rooted in nature" dimension – almost metaphysical – and, second, it maintains real estate values by the meretricious device of canonizing vineyards, making them "immortal", beyond human interference.

Australia
FRUITIEST ISLAND ON EARTH?

"Agatha and I are so much interested in Australia.
It must be so pretty with all the dear little kangaroos flying about."

Oscar Wilde, *Lady Windermere's Fan.*

PREVIOUS PAGE At the end of the rainbow in Margaret River, Western Australia, lies a crock of gold – in the form of vineyards from which come some of the nation's most elegant yet robust wines.

TOP The Clare Valley goes in for less than straightforward vineyards and produces Australia's least straightforward Rieslings. The most curvaceous vineyards are Leasingham's Provis and the Watervale Cemetery's.

BELOW LEFT Out of McLaren Vale comes a Shiraz, from Coriole Estate, which invites comparison, for delicately ruffled richness, with velvet.

BELOW RIGHT Kerri Thompson, winemaker at Leasingham, is behind some of the Clare Valley's most beautifully balanced Shirazes, Cabernet Sauvignons, and Rieslings. Behind her is the plant (*Echium plantagineum*) innocently called by some Salvation Jane, but it is known to livestock farmers as Patersons Curse for it is toxic to horses and grazing animals.

If you thought that dear old Oscar's patronizing attitude towards this vast country merely Victorian disdain, think again. As recently as 1985 things had hardly changed. Around that time the head of the Australian Wine Bureau in London called on the head of wine buying of a major British supermarket, who listened patiently and then said: "You know, I don't think Aussie wines will ever catch on."

Today, we all know how kangaroos get themselves around and every UK wine drinker also knows how Australian wine has got itself about. Indeed, that same supermarket now stocks 170 different Australian wines when twenty years ago it had less than half-a-dozen.

Australian wine makes sense. It talks English: a confident, assertive, unpretentious English that anyone who sees wine as the product of fruit cannot but enjoy. Australian wine is open, warm-hearted, and generous. Old World wine is seen as ritualized, closed up, difficult to get to know, uncool. But Australia has not been content merely to be a fruit machine. It turns out many finely tuned, complex specimens which still manage to express their innate hospitable Australianess.

The country is currently emphasizing how different the wines are from the various States – Western Australia, South Australia, Victoria, Tasmania, New South Wales, and surprise surprise, Queensland. This emphasis does not negate the thesis of this book. On the contrary, it reinforces it. For in a country so massive, where to fly between one region and another can take longer than to fly from London to Moscow, the different climates not only grow different grapes, but different people. And never was a country so cognizant of the fact that wine is not so much a product of a vineyard but of people.

South Australia

This is the pulsating heart of the Australian wine industry and many big-hearted Aussie wines come from here. You might shrug and say but New South Wales has flamboyance, Victoria haughtiness, and Western Australia elegance, but in South Australia, capitalized by prim-yet-delicately-louche Adelaide, you have people with poetry and potency and the wines reflect this.

South Australia has a massive near-67,000 hectares of vineyards (a little over 42 per cent of the Australian total), and it is divided into five zones. These are: Barossa (which includes Eden Valley); Mounty Lofty Ranges (encompassing the Clare Valley, Adelaide Hills, and the Adelaide Plains); Limestone Coast (which takes in Coonawarra, Padthaway, Mount Benson and Robe, Wrattonbully, Koppamurra, and Mount Gambier); Fleurieu (McLaren Vale and Langhorne Creek); and the Lower Murray (Riverland).

Clare Valley

With vegetables

The Aussie sun has grudgingly agreed to come out, though not wholly convincingly. However, by the time the Leasingham winery is reached from my Adelaide hotel, my body casts its first substantial shadow. Ms Kerri Thompson makes the wines here, any shadow of her predecessor, Richard Rowe (who made the very first Aussie reds, so tannicly daring, to set certain UK hearts soaring years back), vanishing quickly as she pours out her own equally challenging vintages. It was Richard who provided, in 1993, my first taste of Australia's raw produce when lunch at this winery consisted of local vegetables (artichokes, asparagus, carrots, potatoes, beetroots, all dressed with local olive oil). This simple but richly flavoursome repast made a deep impression: this was a place where you could grow anything and grow it great.

"I've concentrated on the vines since taking over," Kerri says. "Rod and spur trained them and increased berry size, and as a result the wines have taken a step up in their tannin balance. Also changed the coopers, did some work there."

The European style of handling tannin during the ferment has been adopted, an important component of which is regular pumping over of the cap formed on the top of the wine by the skins. This ensures extraction but not over-extraction. The soil and climate may be perfect for growing grapes, but what the grower does with those grapes is the key factor and Kerri is striving for even greater elegance than Mr Rowe achieved, starting in the vineyard. All winemakers speak their own language; it is only translated, though, when you drink their wines.

There are several bottles to test this theory in the tasting room, starting with the screwcapped Leasingham Bin 7 Riesling. This is tangily complex already (in defiance of its youth), and that screwcap holds out

BELOW LEFT Dave Palmer of Skillogalee vineyard grows artichokes on the side. There's nothing thorny, however, about his wines.

BELOW RIGHT Having just eaten at the Star of Greece restaurant at Willunga, near McLaren Vale, this group of diners is exuberantly happy.

promise for the wine's development and future. Here in Clare one can learn a lot about screwcaps for several prominent local wine producers are now screwcapping their Rieslings, their patience exhausted with cork.

But Kerri has more to show than Riesling. The Sparkling Shiraz is sweetly vibrant, the Classic Clare Cabernet Sauvignon has wonderful tobacco-rich cassis fruit with abundant tannins, the Classic Clare Shiraz is ripe and ready, the Bin 61 Shiraz has cocoa and cassis concentration, the Bin 56 Cabernet/Malbec is playful and plummy, and the cheapest, the ten-bucks-a-bottle Bastion Shiraz/Cabernet Sauvignon offers terrific curry-leaf spice, chocolate, and tobacco, with good tannins.

Knappstein and Skillogalee

Knappstein is a legend in the Valley and the name has been associated with the Riesling grape for many years.

"I like screwcaps," says Andrew Hardy, the winemaker. "I love the fact that you don't have to worry about taint. Just twist off the cap, and there's the wine, fresh and natural." And indeed it is, as his latest wines show with their gritty minerality and concentrated yet subtle fruit.

At Skillogalee estate, owner Dave Palmer seems a living representation of a furry tannin (he sports a beard of Mosaic floribundance). He is a charming man with a charming wife Diane, living an idyllic existence in his heavenly little piece of the Clare. His grapes are turned into wine by son Daniel at their own new winery and it is my bet that within a few years this producer will be turning out not just gritty gewurztraminers and other wines it does now, but world-class Cabernets (as a visit in 2006 confirmed).

Grosset/Mount Horrocks/Wendouree

Grosset is a gold mine, though owner, Jeffrey Grosset, prefers to call it a winery. His lightly golden Rieslings are legendary in the land, the sleekest in Australia. From his Polish Hill vineyard vines he conjures a sublimely minerally and exquisite wine of great finesse, which terroirists will claim owes everything to the complex limestone bases upon which the vineyard sits, but which I believe owes more to Mr Grosset's tender touch and personality. He is a person of great calm and finesse, his resolute beliefs firmly held beneath monastically pale skin which has not seen the sun, it seems, for decades. He is a man of piety and controlled vigour.

He is a highly articulate advocate of screwcaps and both his Grosset Polish Hill Riesling and Watervale Riesling are so sealed. The latter wine is like a fine German Nahe Riesling, with a rich uplift on the finish. The Polish Hill is in a different league, more Rheingau like, with beautifully advanced grapefruit/peach touches, superb acids, and the potential, screwcapped as it is, to develop for thirty years.

"I have forty-six fermentation tanks here so I can pick different vineyard sites, or parts of a vineyard, and vinify separately," he reveals. "One of the secrets of getting consistency in a small winery is doing everything in small batches – and blending."

Not for nothing have some passionate German and French Riesling growers been sufficiently aroused by Jeffrey's wines to visit here: Loosen, Gunderloch, Trimbach, and Breuer amongst them.

"I want the purest expression of the vineyard and its grape," he adds. And one can go along with this because he is prepared to go to enormous lengths to make such things possible. The Riesling is a most expressive grape, more so perhaps than any other; but it is only prepared to reveal its unique charms to those who ferment it lovingly.

With Jeffrey as we taste is Ms Stephanie Toole, who is the owner and winemaker of the neighbouring Mount Horrocks winery. Jeffrey and Stephanie have children together, and he helps make her wines.

Stephanie purchased Mount Horrocks Wines in 1993 when she was "four months pregnant with Georgina and I thought I needed something to keep me busy. I was well and truly pregnant through that first vintage and fifteen months later along came Alexander. I crushed the 1995 vintage fruit four days after he was born. He was beside me in his pram."

Jeffrey leaves for a Wine-growers Association meeting but not before donating a bottle of his 1994 Polish Hill Riesling. This magnificent wine, still excitingly evolving, was part of a unique evening some days later when, off the back of a houseboat on the Murray River, for the first time in my life, after scores of fruitless attempts, I held a fishing rod at the other end of which was a real live fish. I drank that Polish Hill and toasted my catch, a two kilo carp, under the eye of a pelican optimistic of charity. The wine had the aroma of toasted macadamia nuts.

A younger Mount Horrocks Watervale Riesling is not so expressive but it is elegant and fine and, being screwcapped, capable of decades of fit life. "I think," Stephanie says with feeling, "the screwcap is the most exciting thing that's happened in our industry in years. Yet why didn't Penfolds lead the way? Why has it been left to thirteen small Clare Valley producers to take the initiative?"

The Rising Sun Hotel is the dinner venue. This old pub, run by Glenise and John Osborne,[1] is in Auburn a few miles along the road from Clare. Beer-battered snapper and chips partner an eleven-year-old bottle of Wendouree Cabernet/Malbec. The wine is quite wonderful, one of the most honest Aussie reds around. Throwing a crusty sediment (evidence of its considerate handling in the winery and lack of manipulation), it offered cinnamon-edged fruit with a nutty undertone and touches of coffee and chocolate. It had perfect alcohol, 13.5 per cent, in balance with tannins mature and chewy but still persistent, vibrant, couth. Hardly a fish 'n' chip wine? Oh, come on! We're in Australia now. No-rules rules.

Barossa
Gesundheit!
The Barossa Valley is the cradle of the Australian wine industry. Many of the big names are centred here (Penfolds, Yalumba, Wolf Blass, Orlando, even Hardy's has joined in with its new winery). Barossa has an inescapably Germanic atmosphere and in the cemeteries, the churches (Lutheran of course), and even in the rustic architecture of some of the old homesteads and in the quaint castellated design of certain wineries, there is little doubting the provenance of the inhabitants.

No-one can question this Valley's mighty contribution to the Aussie wine miracle. I first saw bush vines here (looking old enough to have known my Austrian grandfather) and heard my first Aussie brass band. Barossa Shiraz is a defining Aussie cultural expression like Bouillabaisse in Marseilles, Highland malt in Aberdeen.

It is in the Barossa that Max Schubert, the legendary Penfolds winemaker, conceived Grange (though it was undoubtedly born in his mind when he was first taken to Bordeaux and marvelled at decades-old reds to which the crafty Bordelais, to his astonishment, were not above adding tannins).

Two early personal favourites from the Barossa, when Aussie wines were parvenus in the UK, were from the Barossa Valley Estate winery in Marananga with its E & E Black Pepper and Ebenezer Shirazes (there was also a brutal Ebenezer Chardonnay). Late 1980s vintages of these wines offered liquids of vigour and uncommon richness. It was, alas, a short-lived dazzlement as the wines seemed quickly to go up three times in price, later vintages to lose their chewy concentration (and a eucalypt liquorice edge). Others more immediately available and rating highly include Bethany, Charles Melton, Glaetzer, Grant Burge, Peter Lehmann, Rockford, Saltram (and Mamre Brook), St Halletts, and Torbreck.

[1] Now calling it a day, alas. The pub is up for sale.

23

This latter estate, in a tasting in early 2005, put an interesting dent in the argument that says the age of the vines is crucial to how good the wine will be. When Torbreck's The Factor 2002 Shiraz (from vines eighty to 120 years old) was compared with The Descedant 2003, from Shiraz vines just nine years old, the former showed remarkable character and rated 17 points out of 20, but The Descendant rated 18. It was magical: full of lively interest, concentrated yet lithe, and with exemplary tannins.

The Barossa is home, amongst many other liquid delights, to Yalumba's superior Viogniers, most of which, with their gamey apricot fruit, put to shame the Rhône originators of this grape (from Condrieu). Orlando also makes its Jacob's Creek wines here, the UK's number one best selling brand; lately the reserve Jacob's Creek, medium-priced, have shown themselves to be serious contenders for anyone's glass. Basedow Semillon is also invariably delicious and Leo Buring Rieslings, with age, can be aromatic masterpieces. Varieties other than the ubiquitous Shiraz can, then, thrive in the Barossa. The most adventurous stab at diversification yet, perhaps, is Ben Glaetzer's Dolcetto and Lagrein marriage, called Heartland. This unites the great red grapes of Piedmont and the Sud-Tirol and the wine has the kind of sublime richness that were one to select a single Aussie wine to introduce to an alien who had never tasted wine before, would offer an excellent starting point. The roasted almond and liquorice fruit of Dolcetto with the crushed mocha coffee-bean tang of Langrein makes for a formidably delicious liquid. Outrageously sensual, the wine stays on the palate like butterscotch.

McLaren Vale
One of the world's great wine regions
The first Aussie wine I ever tasted came from here. It was called Emu Imperial Bounty Ruby Port (sixteen shillings and threepence the bottle

at Gough Brothers in London in 1969, but in the 1950s, when mum kept a bottle under the sink to console the spiders and fortify grandma, it cost half that, and she didn't miss the odd drop). Emu, British owned, was sold to the eponym of the Hardy empire and whatever vineyards supplied the wine are, it is safe to assume, no longer making disgusting copies of European fortified wine, but reds distinctly McLaren Vale in character and fluidity.

Nowadays Australian reds can sit down at the same table as the wines they once looked up to – and be superior. An example is where the Syrah (or Shiraz) grape has been blended, as in Côte Rôtie in the Rhône, with a little of the white grape Viognier. Many drinkers are surprised to learn that one of France's greatest reds is partially vinified with white grapes. It is not, though, a blend. *Appellation contrôlée* rules stipulate that a winemaker cannot blend Viognier wine with Syrah but can only vinify the two varieties together as grapes; whereas in McLaren Vale, or anywhere else in Australia for that matter, the two can be combined at any stage. Once, after several days spent as a judge at the McLaren Vale wine show, I tasted Aussie Shiraz/Viognier blends alongside their French counterparts.

The Roos:
Kangarilla Road Shiraz/Viognier:
Soft with ripe tannins, amazingly mature feel for a youthful wine. 17/20
Cobaw Ridge Syrah/Viognier:
Lacks structure, sweet on the finish. 14/20
Heathcote Victorian Shiraz/Viognier:
Still a bit raw and uncomfortably tannic. 14.5/20
D'Arenburg The Laughing Magpie Shiraz/Viognier:
Superb! Great balance of elements and lovely tannins. 18/20

LEFT One tradition the Hardy Wine Company of Reynella, McLaren Vale, never lets die is the imaginative use of typography, elegant yet striking, on its labels.

RIGHT The cliffs near Australia's oldest nudist beach, Maslin, a few miles from McLaren Vale, expose evidence of the great antiquity of the whole island's surface geology.

SOUTH AUSTRALIA

25

TOP Barrels outside Wirra Wirra Winery in McLaren Vale represent a huge investment in wood technology. Barrels are a major influence on the style of a wine.

BELOW Ed Carr, sparkling winemaker for Hardy's, understands the secret of his trade: blending. Single-vineyard bubbly is rare compared to the blended variety, for it is only by blending wines from different vineyards, and often different grapes, that a true classic sparkling wine can emerge.

The Frogs:
La Mouline Côte Rôtie Guigal:
*Touch of sulphur not good, bit raw for eight years old, tannins like hacksaw
blades. 14/20*
La Landonne Côte Rôtie Guigal:
*No Viognier here, just 100 per cent Syrah (I think), but great leathery tannins
and a touch of sweetness on the finish. 16/20*
Côte Rôtie La Turque Côte Brune Guigal:
What vigour for such an age! Amazingly vibrant tannins. 17/20

Evidence, if any is needed, that the Emu is well and truly extinct.

Vintage Carr, Wirra Wirra
At Hardy's Reynella winery, where Emu once ruled, many fine
basket-pressed reds are made, but also bubblies. Sparkling winemaker
Ed Carr, in his dazzlingly pristine tasting room, carefully assembles (the
truly creative endeavour of bubbly making being the blending) some
lively wines.

These include Yarra Burn Pinot Noir/Chardonnay/Pinot Meunier,
Starve Dog Lane Adelaide Hills Chardonnay/Pinot Noir/Pinot Meunier,
Omni, and Arras. This latter wine is considered one of Australia's top
bubblies. It has a delicious toasty richness.

But so does, amazingly, a thirty-year-old "Rhine Riesling" taken from
Hardy's museum stock. The wine is lime-scented and rich: hale, healthy,
delicious. How come? It is screwcapped.

As is Wirra Wirra's Riesling. What sounds like a Gaelic curse is in fact
the name of this top McLaren Vale winery, producer of a most emphatic
range of wines. The Riesling is young and feisty, but give it a couple of
years under that screwcap and it'll be even finer. Other wines here also
show themselves to be thought-provoking experiences.

Sexton's Acre Unwooded Chardonnay is ripe, immature, yet complex.
Scrubby Rise Semillon/Sauvignon Blanc/Chardonnay has a vivid aroma.
Scrubby Rise Semillon/Sauvignon Blanc/Viognier shows smoky peach
fruit. A young Wirra Wirra Chardonnay is already oily and elegant and,
most gracious of all, a magnificent older Wirra Wirra Chardonnay
parades brilliantly integrated wood with elegant, vegetal fruit. And that's
just the whites.

The Scrubby Rise Shiraz/Cabernet Sauvignon/Petit Verdot has lush
tannins. Church Block Cabernet Sauvignon/Shiraz/Merlot shows more
tarry tannins. Wirra Wirra McLaren Vale Shiraz has intense tannins. RSW
Shiraz, three years old but wise in the head, has burned tannins. The
Angelus Cabernet Sauvignon, a blend of McLaren Vale and Coonawarra
fruit, has minerally tannins. Vineyard Series Coonawarra Cabernet
Sauvignon has tannins like velvet. Wirra Wirra must be local dialect for
Tannins! Tannins!

Trio at Coriole

At Coriole Vineyards winemaker Grant Harrison, Mark Lloyd (whose business card modestly proclaims him to be the general manager, but who owns the joint), and the new viticulturalist Rachel Steer lay on a tasting. This, planned alfresco, has been hastily transferred under an awning because the rain, impressive in its learning-curve, has matured from yesterday's British-type shower and blossomed into a full-on oriental monsoon.

Having already experienced that gorgeous Coriole Lloyd Reserve Shiraz at The Star of Greece (restaurant), the people who make it strike me with equal force of personality and character. Rachel may have been in the job only a few months, but I know why Mark and Grant hired her: she shares the same soul (and similar richly expressive eyes).

Coriole produces deeply felt wines because the people growing them feel deeply. This produces in the wine critic one of those dilemmas stubborn of resolution. Can one judge wines objectively if you feel so warm towards their makers? This is the great seductive trap which awaits the critic of wine (or of anything else for that matter): fall for the people behind the wine (book, film, restaurant, concerto) and you'll never see the product clearly because the critical faculties have been blurred, blunted. What is in the bottle is no longer just a liquid, just vinified fruit, but a person or people.

Mark Lloyd pours Shirazes from the 1995, 1996, 1997, 1998, and 1999 vintages. The 1997 has a remarkable smokiness and spicy tannins, the 1998 actually has the tang of cardamom. Goodness, what wonderful fruit is here in each wine, with great structure and elegance. These are exceptional wines in anyone's book. The top-end stuff at Coriole is truly top drawer.

The Sangiovese and Nebbiolo are also fine and one is struck, in each case, by not only the overwhelming varietal fidelity of the wines, but their superiority to their Italian counterparts in all but the finest examples of the latter. Mark quizzed me about the Fiano grape from Naples (he has a thing about Italian culture, including opera) when we first met. By 2006, the Fiano vines were in production, turning out a nutty specimen of genteel richness less subtle than its Neopolitan counterpart but equally as alluring.

The Fiano grape, which makes Fiano di Avellino, the Neopolitan's greatest white wine, is an imaginative addition to the Coriole canon. It also provides another reason why Australia has so shaken up France: its winemakers are free to experiment. In AOC areas of France, the winemakers have to put their hands up if they want to visit the lavatory during the harvest. They are only allowed to plant permitted grape varieties on the precious appellation controlled hectares, no others (though they can legally add sugar, derived from beet, to their musts, to raise alcohol levels – a practice, called chaptalisation, which pollutes the purity of what terroir allegedly stands for).

After Coriole, Serafino makes an immediate impression because of the winery's newness. As well as a winery, Serafino is also a resort hotel and conference centre behind which is Steve Maglieri who, having flogged his Maglieri winery and estate for shed loads of money, has put some of it into this latest McLaren Vale venture.

Winemaker Scott Rawlinson is making excellent commercial wines, comprising an unwooded Chardonnay and a "top end" McLaren Vale Shiraz. Both perfectly match the unpretentious exuberance of their maker. When Scott's wife Donna arrives, as the tasting ends, the Rawlinsons take me to see Australia's first nude beach, Maslin. More dramatic than any unclad human, the beach features limestone cliffs, much eroded and disfigured, and spectacularly striated with marble, limestone, and basalt. This remarkable littoral architecture, when the sun is up and the shadows are like pools of thickened blood, is worth the detour.

Coonawarra
Does the answer lie in the soil?
Invariably impressive wines from here have been Katnook, Penley Estate, Hollick, Rymill, Balnaves, Yalumba, Jamiesons Run, and the wonderful old Cabernets, made by winemaker Sue Hodder's predecessors, at Wynns Coonawarra Estate. If any region in Australia stands a chance of refuting the notion that terroir is more important than the individual who farms it, it is this one. Coonawarra's famed *terra rossa* soil, which lies atop a massive limestone subsoil, is visually impressive, but all the wineries mentioned each make their wines in more or less the same way, which is why they each present similar personality traits.

The subsoil is claimed to some of the Cabernets – mostly notably Wynns', now and then, in some vintages – a certain minerally mintiness. But as it is not widespread, it seems to me a fugitive characteristic. Besides, are the eucalyptus trees near the vines not to blame for the minty undertone of some of the Cabernets?

Does the soil, however, confer longevity? Something in Coonawarra does. In London in 2005 Sue Hodder opened Wynns Coonawarra Cabernet Sauvignons from 1954 through to 2004. Twenty-five wines, all in combative nick, and though the older ones showed some wrinkling, it was amazing to taste a robust wine from 1954 – the year Betty and Phil first made a State visit to Oz and Roger Banninster ran a mile in under four minutes. The 1960 was more impressive, with the Coonawarra mintiness and fulsome tannins. The 1976 showed coffee and chocolate. The 1992 was back to more After Eight mintiness. All in all, a convincing demonstration that Aussie Cabernets can age as gracefully as anyone's (and be more like Cabernet than most).

New South Wales

In the ten years between the mid-1990s and the six-year-old new millennium the hectarage of vines in this region increased by a little short of 250 per cent. This is, in a way, the story of the whole dynamic Aussie wine scene, though NSW actually accounts for less than 24 per cent of the national total of vines. However, in its Hunter Valley – home to those fabulous, spiky, long-lived Semillons – it has the most internationally recognized wine tourist destination in the country and one of Australia's top tourist attractions (Sydney Opera House, eat your heart out). The Hunter is the most famous, yes, but some of the fourteen other designated wine areas – Murray Darling, Swan Hill (not to be confused with Swan District in Western Australia), Perricoota, Riverina, Hasting River, Shoalhaven Coast, Sydney Basin, Southern Highlands, Tumbarumba, Canberra District, Hilltops, Cowra, Orange, and Mudgee – are well worth investigating. Therein lies about 150 producers all told, give or take a couple. Most are well worth the taking.

Orange

What sort of man calls his dog Pimp?

Stephen Doyle of Bloodwood Wines is a man with a sense of humour as deliciously prickly as his beard. He likes naming things (he was a librarian, so taxonomic gestures are built into his psyche). One of his wines is called Schubert; another, a bubbly, Chirac. The origins of the former name are banal, but Chirac, commemorating the great survivor of French politics, has fans at the French embassy who enjoy drowning their sorrows in bottles of Chirac (a wily blend of Pinot Noir and Chardonnay which rated 17.5 points out of 20 at thirty bucks the bottle).

The beautifully smooth yet characterful Shiraz rated 18 points, the lovely strawberry-edged Pinot Noir 16 points, the lean, complex Schubert Chardonnay 17.5 points. Only the Merlot proved difficult to like as much.

Bloodwood is one of those intensely individual vineyard set-ups – the word winery seems out-of-place here, since Stephen and Rhonda's wines

are manifestly the products of people rather than a manufactory. They are amongst the hidden glories of Australian viticulture and, more importantly, culture generally.

Lower Hunter Valley
Tradition – like father like son like Semillon
The Lower Hunter Valley has become a major tourist destination. In good years, some 1.5 million tourists swan through here, tasting wine, playing golf, eating the local food. One destination for many of them is Tyrrell's – "Australian family-owned since 1858", as it proudly proclaims. It is now one of Australia's top twenty wine companies, since it produces wines from other regions than its native Hunter.

Mark Richardson, the winemaker, creates a lean style of wine. It's the Semillons which stand out, reflecting the Tyrrell personality (the honied sentimentality restrained by a dry, subtly burned-hay undertone). Tyrrell's Semillons are the pioneers of the European style of this wine in the Hunter. It results in wines which can often give much-vaunted white burgundies (made of course from a different grape altogether, Chardonnay) a run for their considerably greater money. In some vintages, a lack of clarity on the finish is detectable when young, as if the wine has something else on its mind by the time it gets to the back of the throat. However, given five or six years of bottle age, these Semillons often sort themselves out with aplomb. In February 2005, at Sydney's Royal Wine Show, Tyrrell's 1997 Vat 1 Semillon was awarded the trophy for Best Wine of all the entrants. Bruce Tyrrell remarked, "If you added up the regions and their varietals, Hunter Semillon was so far ahead. I think next was Riesling from Clare."

Two men in a beard
The Hunter's bearded double act is Greg West and John Rogers of McWilliams. Greg sports a splendid King Edward set of whiskers with upturned ends to his 'tache, whereas John, being a local JP, has more discrete hirsute decorations which amply compensate for the glabrous donnishness of his brow. This is a big company with big ambitions. It is the fifth largest winery operation in the country and wholly family owned.

McWilliams, apart from its Hunter Mount Pleasant winery and vineyards, also operates two big wineries in Griffiths, one in Lilydale in the Yarra, one in Redvale, one in Robinvale (Victoria), and one in Coonawarra, as well as taking fruit from contract growers in Western Australia and the Clare, Barossa, and Eden valleys. The Mount Pleasant Pinot Noir has most attractive tannins.

The most striking wine here, though, is the Mount Pleasant Elizabeth Semillon, with its vibrant acids. Hunter Semillons get into a flighty fecundity of acidity around five years of age – the paradox of which is a lean straw-edged effect – which marks out the best of this region's style with this grape. In the local Lovedale Semillon this delicious paradox is also richly evident. "The soil's so poor at the Lovedale vineyard," says John, delivering this insight with the practised authority he doubtless brings when passing judgements on motorists caught speeding, "the rabbits carry lunchboxes."

Grab and run (to the garrulous guru)

Iain Riggs from Brokenwood, home of the exquisite Graveyard Shiraz, demonstrates the generosity of Aussies. He does not wish to take his visitor on a tour of his winery or his vineyards. He wants to take me on a tour of a local monument, wine celebrity Len Evans. Mr Evans is a former journalist who made his pile when the Rothbury Estate winery he developed was bought by Mildara Blass in 1988. With Mr Evans no longer its inspirational driving force, Rothbury wines lack his ebullient personality; Mr Evans consoles himself in his house, set on a gentle knoll replete with startling garden statuary where he can sit and scowl at his ex-winery in the vale below.

Mr Evans pours a 1974 Hunter Shiraz (no label), a 1989 Rothbury Syrah, a 1990 Huntington Mudgee Cabernet Sauvignon/Merlot, and a 1998 Penfolds Bin 389 Cab/Shiraz. The Bin 389, Len announces (it's got to Len by then), will last for twenty or thirty years.

His feathers ruffle as the question is raised as to whether the wine's cork could possibly support such a future: "I'm a consultant for Amorim," he says (the large Portuguese cork manufacturer which has hired Len to espouse its cause in Australia). "So I'm prejudiced in favour of cork. I'm a fan of cork. I think screwcaps are an excellent seal," he adds: "But a great wine will never reach its peak under a screwcap."

"What about bottle variation?" the visitor asks. He sighs. "Bottle variation, Malcolm, is all part of the charm of wine."

From Meerea to Scarborough by way of Allandale and Wyndham

Garth Eather (who, like his brother Rhys, is a bear of a man who exudes the genteel restraint of a mouse), is unequivocal about screwcaps. "Anyone who makes an aromatic white and doesn't screwcap it is an idiot," he says and proceeds to pour his Meerea Park wines.

Meerea Park wines reflect the Eathers' personalities absolutely. Which is to say the wines are large and furry with soft hearts (and don't show their claws). Admirable are an Epoch Semillon, a Lindsay Hill Verdelho, an Orchard Road Pinot Gris from Orange (in a screwcap, so give the wine ten years and it'll be even feistier), Orchard Road Barbera from Orange, a terrific The Aunt's Shiraz, and a very accomplished Shiraz/Viognier.

They present a cohesive front in spite of the varied provenance of the fruit which has made them. "The best way to describe our business," says Rhys, "is to think of it as like a high quality Burgundy négociant's." Just like other successful wineries in the Hunter, Meerea Park doesn't just rely on local-grown grapes, but on out-sourcing fruit from other regions and makes a variety of styles. The dog at Rhys's feet, Baerami, is also a Meerea Park blend, being a striking mixture of Rhodesian Ridgeback, Labrador, and German Shepherd.

Karl Stockhausen is purer bred with a gentle German accent though he's been a local for fifty years and is an Aussie. He is the consultant for the Allandale winery and today filling in for the winemaker, Bill Sneddon, who is on holiday (the explanation given, though he may have been in hiding). This is another set-up sourcing fruit from several areas: the Hunter, Mudgee, Hilltops, McLaren Vale, Orange, and Hastings River.

The best wine was a marvellously crisp and nutty Semillon. A Verdelho was also interesting with cellaring potential. The Chardonnay and Chardonnay blends were less coherent. The reds featured a pious Shiraz, called rather appropriately Matthew: whether its finish was subtle or just plain mean was difficult to decide. Other reds, from Mudgee and Hilltops, strained to greater effect and showed dusty oak edges.

Wyndham Estate, part of the Orlando-Wyndham conglomerate (of Jacob's Creek fame) now owned by Pernod Ricard, is a somewhat grander operation. The winery, first built in 1828, is the only one on the banks of the Hunter River itself. Penfolds once owned it but sold out because the river once flooded and half-drowned the place. Wyndham now hosts opera festivals where the river burst its banks.

Brett McKinnon, chief winemaker, announces: "'The Big Australian Taste' is our advertising strapline, so I'm not going to make a lean wine."

Attaboy. And he is true to his anti-Weight-Watchers word. Tasting twenty-nine of his wines one finds none is lean. There's a fat and flowery sparkling Chardonnay; a Show Reserve Semillon, of which the most challenging vintage was a nine year-old with its waxy apricot fruit and medicinal, Islay malt whisky undertone; two Bin 222 Chardonnays; a Bin 111 Verdelho; a pungent Show Reserve Chardonnay; a quiet Bin 333 Pinot Noir; a NV Bin 555 Sparkling Shiraz, dry but fruity; a Bin 999 Merlot from fruit grown in Mudgee, Riverina, and Langhorne Creek; a rousing Bin 444 Cabernet; plus a line-up of rich, fruity Shirazes.

With Ian Scarborough, we're back among the small producers. With his wife Merralea, Ian owns the Scarborough Wine Company. Jerome, the son, is the general manager; daughter Sally responsible for sales and marketing in Victoria and Queensland. It does not, however (cosy family considerations aside), sound promising. With a name like this it sounds like an off-licence in Yorkshire.

In fact, Scarborough is a wine producer in the meaningful sense of the word. It owns just forty hectares of vines and though it makes a little Semillon and Shiraz, it specializes in Chardonnay and Pinot Noir. Given the grapes, Burgundy springs to mind, but on tasting the wines any comparison quickly fades. These wines are much sexier than your average white or red burgundy.

The Pinot Noir comprises fruit grown on just under a hectare of Scarborough soils so this is not a wine which will find its way out of Oz (since not much more than 500 cases are made). The Chardonnays are made in two styles: Yellow Label has more butteriness and French oak intrusion; Blue Label is fresher and more citrousy. Both are excellent, but the Blue Label style with its sinuous acidity and elongated citricity is the more elegant. The Semillon was stunning, truly exceptional, clean and lemony: lean, lanky Hunter Semillon at its purest expression. Equally straightforward, uncomplicated, and unpretentious is Ian Scarborough himself. His wines, even his funky Pinot Noir, are forceful expressions of the man.

"We're making wines to be drunk within three years of being made," he says. "I think that generally within a year of being sold that's as good as they're going to get."

What? None of the regulation blarney about the wines being okay to cellar for twenty-five years? One breathes fresh air at Scarborough. This stimulant to appetite is taken to Shakey Tables restaurant to meet Jerome and his wife and eat a boned wood pigeon stuffed with blood sausage and prunes. In typical generous Aussie fashion Ian insists a Tyrrell's Semillon is served alongside his own as an apéritif and finds it incredible that his guest pronounces Scarborough to be in the same class as Tyrrell's or even a touch tangier. He seems disappointed. Where else in the world would a winemaker present you with a rival's wine and be disappointed you found his own one more exciting? Equally generously, Ian also produces a fulsome, liquorice-tinged Barwang Cabernet Sauvignon (a McWilliams wine), from the tiny Hilltops area which has just six producers.

Anyone who is thinking of visiting the Lower Hunter Valley must not delay. Visit Scarborough before a giant wine conglomerate buys it for AUS$30 million (£12.7 million) and a burger corporation acquires Shakey Tables and turns it into a worldwide bistro chain. Neither prospect is remotely on the cards, but who knows? The Lower Hunter was once full of sheep and men swinging scythes. Now it's full of tourists and men swinging golf clubs.

Trust me – I'm a doctor

Doctor Phillip Norrie is a Sydney GP and he's also an amateur historian. His other major preoccupations are wine and health – and his own vineyard, Pendarves Estate in the Lower Hunter. The wines show little of the owner's personality because the winemaking is contracted out.

A day spent in his company is inspiring. "I have an idea how you can write this up," the good doctor says, his rotund features and cheerful bald head nodding vigorously as he speaks. We're at the Harbour restaurant in the Hyatt hotel enjoying Tim Gramp's Watervale Riesling and the superb views of the Opera House. "You can say that you've had a drink facing the site of Australia's first vineyard.[1] Right there. You see? Just up from the Quays, on that slope about where the Intercontinental hotel now is."

[1] Established in 1788, when Captain Arthur Phillip founded Port Jackson, as Sydney was once called.

In the Upper Hunter Valley
...with Rosemount

Though the Hunter Valley is officially one region, it is divided into Upper and Lower. The Upper, with around a dozen producers, is the home of Rosemount wines – drunk all over the world, but not all made from Hunter fruit. The most accomplished are Hill of Gold Chardonnay, Diamond Label Shiraz, Rosemount Estate Traditional Shiraz (showing solid McLaren Vale tannins), and Show Reserve Shiraz, made not in the Upper Hunter but at the Rycroft winery in McLaren Vale.

Mudgee
Hilltop hideaway

You might be familiar with McLaren Vale and Barossa, perhaps even the Margaret River and Coonawarra, but Mudgee, tucked away in the foothills of the Great Dividing Range, needs a little introducing. Mudgee became a gold region in the 1850s and twenty years later the world's largest nugget of gold, weighing 286 kilograms, was unearthed here. At the time it was valued at an awesome £15,000. The poet Henry Lawson was also born in the gold fields. Lawson, his poetic style like Fennimore Cooper re-written by Richmal Crompton, became the first Aussie writer to be given a state funeral when he died in 1922.

As a wine region Mudgee was, like the Barossa, set up by German settlers and some of the first Chardonnay to be produced in Australia was planted here. By 1880 it had a dozen or so wineries and around 162 hectares of vines. The region declined and by 1962 there was only one winery left. In the past decade and a half, though, Mudgee, a town of some 8,500 people, a four-hour drive from Sydney, has regenerated itself.

It has three dozen wine producers nowadays and none excites more than Huntington Estate. Its wines show an elegance tempered by an undercurrent of boisterous richness wholly echoed by owner Bob Roberts (who drives a 1970 Mercedes 3.9SL, with electric windows, automatic steering column shift stick, and leather seats). Why do his wines never appear on the UK market? "Well, I did export to the UK," he says. "But I didn't get paid very frequently so..."

Huntington wines are not, then, seen as much overseas as they might. Nor would they be widely distributed in any event, for this is a modest estate, some forty hectares of vines, and therefore only a small number of cases could ever be made available for export. The wines are predominantly found in Sydney restaurants and Aussie bottle shops. (Sydney consumes 45 per cent of Australia's domestic wine for it is, with its 4,000,000 people, by far the largest stomach on the island).

Huntingdon wines are enthralling. Even the cheaper (AUS$12.50/£5.30) Semillon, which Bob calls Château Cash Flow, is impressive. However, it is the reds that demand respect – they have a tenacity of focus which is rare (as I discover when an ancient bottle of the estate's Cabernet Sauvignon shines at dinner even after a hair-raising journey of some hours).

"We've always kept in mind the great wines of France," says Bob. "We go for longevity." This is longevity is evident when tasting the wines. The 1999, 1997, 1995, 1994, 1993, 1991, 1989, and 1982 Shirazes, and Cabernets of 2000, 1999, 1998, 1997, 1995, 1982, and 1979 show themselves with not a dud among the lot. The Shirazes have subtle liquorice touches, some chocolate; the Cabernets spice and herbs. The tannins, untouched by fining (which can strip out personality), are full and sinuous.

The wines are dark, hairy, rich, abundantly berried masterpieces of Mahler-like melancholy with a Mozartian undertone of joyousness. Schubertian is the word which springs to mind. These metaphors may seem extravagant, but are not lightly made. The estate is serious about wine and serious about music. It hosts an annual music festival, since winemaker daughter Susie is also Mrs Richard Tognetti, wife of the director of the Australian Chamber Orchestra.

"Schubert touches me more than any other composer," remarks Bob as his parting shot. Who needs terroir when you have Schubert to inspire you? It was Jonathan Swift, I think, who remarked of a wine that it was too good to be drunk, but must be eaten, and some of Huntington's Cabernets are such wines.

(In early 2006, Bob Roberts sold Huntingdon Estate to neighbours Tim and Connie Stevens of Abercorn Wines).

Harmonica music

Andrew Harris Vineyards in Mudgee is to be discovered perched on a hillock with a good view of Mount Frome (a modest 800 metres/2,625 feet high). Between the modern winery and the mountain is the Harris home, a renovated, rebuilt sheep station. Before there were vines here there were only sheep. Andrew Harris Vineyards is young and thrusting, established in 1991. After tasting half-a-dozen wines in the winery with winemaker Frank Newman, who was born in Lancashire, one is forced to conclude that the wines are some five or six vintages away from true outstanding richness and structured finesse. There was a woodiness of tannins tending to overshadow the fruit which will be less vibrant once the tannins have softened.

These wines are the complete antithesis, at present, of the previous producer. Harris wines represent music played on a harmonica, with all the rawness of sound and simplicity that the comparison evokes. Within two vintages, I would anticipate the addition of percussion and sax. A Cabernet/Merlot showed this potential, as did the Vision Shiraz.

If I sound lazily critical, I mean only to point up the excitement that these wines, if Frank is given his head (which includes putting some if not all the wines in screwcaps), could generate when the vines acquire some leafy wisdom and the roots some experience of life. There is no doubt in my mind that Andrew loves the land and Frank the vines. He is a very experienced, down-to-earth, feet-on-the-ground winemaker who may, at this estate, one day produce wines to drool over.

Queensland

There are, as Benjamin Disraeli eloquently put it, "lies, damned lies and statistics." In this regard, it can be said, without contradiction, that this state contains somewhat less than 1.5 per cent of the country's vines. However, since the majority of these are for table grapes that statistic gives a most misleading picture of Queensland's importance as a wine producer. In fact, the state's contribution to Australian viticulture probably amounts to no more than 0.33 per cent of the national total of grapes crushed for wine. Queensland is divided into four areas, Granite Belt, South Burnett, Queensland Coastal, and Queensland Zone, and boasts just about fifty producers.

Granite Belt, South Burnett
A first for British wine journalism

This requires a trek and commitment. One flies from London to Sydney, thence Brisbane, and hires a car (in my case, in fact, a Ka). One pauses for refreshment and beach games at Noosa Heads, an exquisite resort highly recommended for its food and amiable locals, and then motors for two hours through Eumundi, Cooroy, Gympie, Woolooga, Kilkivan, and Goomeri to Murgon. This brings you to South Burnett and the Clovely Estate where Gerald Keatinge and Mark Kleimeyer, directors of the company, congratulate their visitor on not only finding the place, but being the first British wine writer to have visited the vineyards hereabouts. This is frontier country wine-wise, requiring a frontier spirit (and money if you want to establish a commercial vineyard).

And as you spit out the wines (in to a handy tasting-room spittoon), there are local inhabitants keen to spit back. South Burnett brought me face to face with my first Brown snake, a disagreeable five-foot critter with venom sufficient to kill 200 mice instantaneously and a human in minutes.

Clovely's wines are less intimidating and competently made, but unexciting, the fruit is happiest with oriental food. But then this is a young estate. It has yet to get much of its output into Queensland restaurants let alone the UK. On the evidence of one wine, Frog Chardonnay, there is no doubt it can achieve elegance and style here one day and perhaps surprise the rest of Australia's wine regions which look down on Queensland as a brash parvenu.

The wines made by Stuart Pierce at Barambah Ridge show no such rawness. His Verdelho is tangily superb and his oaked Chardonnay very stylishly structured.

This could not be said of the area's peanut wine (the local town, Kingaroy, is Australia's peanut capital). And John Crane, who makes this unique specimen at Crane winery, has much more interesting liquids still, which include a wine made from jaboticaba berries, a kind of wild grape with a texture not unlike lychee.

ALL THE ABOVE Annie Medhurst, cellar hand at Crane winery, cleans out the press. The wine being made here is from jaboticaba berries, unique to this winery (as is its peanut wine). John Crane's Shirazes are more conventional, though still mightily individual. He also makes a toothsome sweet Muscat from Frontignac grapes.

His grape wines, though, are altogether formidable liquids. The Shirazes are meaty with a bitter cherry richness and a faint liquorice undertone and they have attractive tannins. There is also an impressive sweet Frontignac, a remarkably multi-layered wine of some class.

Making wine from peanuts and jaboticaba berries is nothing to Ross Whiteford, of Stuart Range Estates, as he is making wine from an old cheese factory (it's been a winery only since 1997). A Chardonnay, a Merlot, and several Shirazes create an impression, but mostly of better things to come.

Captain's Paddock Vineyards, named after the horse which lives adjacent to the vines, has Ross make its wines. It has a charming 11% ABV Shiraz which must be Australia's lightest.

Other decisive Queensland wines include a fine Verdehlo from Robert Channon, a Symphony Hill Reserve Cabernet Sauvignon, and Sirromet Chardonnnay and Semillon.

Western Australia

Steel-hearted wines, like the people – slow to anger, gradual in maturity, solid, rural and elegant, nothing showy or shallow – keep their own counsel, take 'em as you find 'em. If that sounds more like a description of the Nantaise in the Loire or the Sud-Tirolese in northern Italy, it is no coincidence as the people and the vines of all three enjoy dramatic, often chilly, climates. WA's is a small vineyard region, pushing 12,000 hectares (less than eight per cent of Australia's total), but its influence, due to the singularity of its Shirazes and Chardonnays, Rieslings and Semillons, not to mention the blends, is great. Its two zones, Greater Perth and Southwest Australia, comprise seven regions: Swan Valley; Perth Hills; Geographe; Margaret River; Blackwood Valley; Pemberton; and Great Southern.

Great Southern (Mount Barker)

Pom undeterred

It is easy to pass for English in this part of the world in October. You wear shorts. An innocent at large? Yes indeed. Spring by the Southern Ocean is bracing.

Mount Barker is basking under not just bruised but seriously battered skies, the local population dressed for an Aberdonian winter. Consider this Australia? No. Consider, instead, this one reason why the wines from this area are so compelling and taken seriously. Even Mount Barker's high school has a vineyard of its own.

It is in this high school that the annual wine show is held. Wine shows are an integral and crucially important part of the all-Australia

LEFT There are few more sublime pairings than a Western Australian Semillon from Cullen and a rock lobster from the Southern Ocean.

RIGHT There is a quaint, old-fashioned side to odd corners of Western Australia. The caravan, though, is purely ornamental. There was no-one in when I knocked.

wine scene. No region, or even subregion (like Mount Barker, which is just a small part of Great Southern) is without one; they attract hundreds of entries from local wineries, and competition is fierce. There are also big city wine events where wines from all the regions can be submitted – these are the most prestigious and the awards the most coveted. The scoring system is rational, yet open to internal debate, and there is exactly the right balance of discussion and individual input. If Australia did not take these shows so seriously – and they are taken so by everyone in the industry – then the eminent position Aussie wines have nowadays in the world market would simply not exist. It is through these shows that wine styles have developed, expertise has been passed on, quality enhanced, and a rapid learning curve negotiated.

After the judges have deliberated, the entries are laid out for locals to taste. For me, one red wine stands out. It is number 33 in Class 20. It turns out to be Jack Mann Cabernet Sauvignon/Malbec (hardly truly local, as it is made by Hardy's at the Houghton winery near Perth 300 kilometres/186 miles north). Truly local, Great Southern region wines which have impressed me include Howard Park with its inexpensive but classy Madfish label, Alkoomi Rieslings, Plantagenet with its Omrah unoaked Chardonnay, and Frankland Estate (Riesling and a Bordeaux blend).

The chairman of judges, Dr John Gladstones, makes a speech. He refers to the "different climatic areas" within the region of Western Australia, but offers no evidence as to how these different areas will affect the smell and taste of the various wines. "What is the Manjimup style of Shiraz going to be...?" he muses and I can tell him: it will be regionally distinctive in its cool climate acids boosting the tannins, but thereafter it'll merely be Western Australian (given a decent winemaker).

John Hanley, chief judge, now speaks, remarking that "this could become the Provence of Australia". The thickly sweatered crowd concurs, many pasty-faced heads nodding (fearful of skin cancer, many Aussies avoid the sun – a search for evidence of the latter outside the gym's misty, rain-scarred windows reveals nothing). Mr Hanley is clearly not referring to the Provence last seen in the south of France. The speeches wind up and the trophy is won by Larry Cherubino (who has since gone to work at the Craggy Range winery in Hawkes Bay, New Zealand), maker of wine 33, Class 20.

Referring to local potential, the Australian wine commentator and winemaker, James Halliday, wrote (in 1998): "Western Australia is definitely the place to be." Not in October, James. Not in October.

Margaret River
Knee exposure ended
At Winos restaurant, octopus and gnocchi disappear with a bottle of wonderfully grouchy, opinionated Moss Wood Cabernet Sauvignon (the same winery's Semillon would have been more apt, but less warming).

Next morning shorts are abandoned for thick chinos. A sweater goes over a plaid shirt. Cape Mentelle, when reached, is not yet open to visitors, but one can admire the gaggle of haughty geese which keep the vineyard clear of snails. Dave Hohnen has run an immaculate estate here for years and his Shirazes, Cabernet Sauvignons, Cabernet/Merlots, and Chardonnays dazzle. Equally, so do Leeuwin Estate's fabulous Chardonnays, Cullen's deft Cabernet/Merlots, Moss Wood's Exotic Semillon and complex Cabernet Sauvignon, and Vasse Felix's delicious Chardonnays and Shirazes. What makes these estates so outstanding? The Margaret River location is extraordinary, the area most dramatically maritime in all of Australia; thus the grapes get plenty of abundant sunshine during the growing season along with chilly nights. As the sugars revel by day, the acids develop by night – all that is needed to coax brilliance from the berries' resultant complexities is an inspirational, consistently attentive, and creative winemaker. And in Dave Hohnen, Vanya Cullen, Bob Cartwright, Keith Mugford, and Clive Otto respectively, those four estates have that advantage.

Pierro must also be mentioned here. This small estate – under 8,000 cases a year – has a dynamic proprietor and winemaker in Michael Peterkin. His Chardonnay has proved a combative and decisive component of several meals in the UK. I am indebted to James Halliday for the insight that "Dr Michael Peterkin makes wines in his own image, complex and concentrated...". It would be this book's contention that a serious wine cannot help but reflect its maker's personality. Also producing lovely Rieslings is Capel Vale (in the Geographe area).

Tasmania

This large island south of Victoria has its hero, Dr Andrew Pirie of Piper's Brook vineyards (finesse not power being the key to the wines in spite of Dr Pirie selling out to Kreglinger, a Belgian company). Of the island's sparkling wines I have been especially fond of Taltarni's Clover Hill and Jansz (part of Yalumba). Indeed, the latter bubbly, at a blind tasting held at Australia House on London's Strand in 2005, outpointed Champagnes such as Pommery, Mumm, Perrier-Jouët, Laurent-Perrier, Taittinger, Veuve Clicquot, Moët & Chandon, and Mercier, as well as other Aussie bubblies such as Seppelt, Grant Burge, Croser, Green Point, and Yering Station. The Jansz was rich yet elegant: the classiest set of bubbles on offer.

Around eighty producers divided into seven regions make up Tasmania which has been a significant wine producer only since the 1970s. The regions are Tamar Valley, North West, Piper's Brook, East Coast, Coal River, Derwent Valley and Southern. Whether any differences between a Tamar and a Derwent Cabernet Sauvignon are climatic or the result of winemaking practices is beyond my current knowledge to speculate.

Victoria

This is the hoity-toitiest of Aussie wine states. The Melbournians are more stiff-upper-lipped than Sydneysiders, less unbuttoned than Adelaidians; they pout more than the inhabitants of Perth. They wear their Australianness as certain individuals wear silk socks; as if only they can appreciate the luxury of the adornment. Anthony Trollope in his travelogue of Australia (1873) felt more at home here than anywhere in Oz on the grounds that there was a piano in every parlour with someone who knew how to play, and shelves lined with books he would care to read. The wines have an intellectual quality too. They provoke by their mannerliness rather than rouse by their potency. The textures caress, the perfumes tickle rather than overpower; they have an assured though subtle swagger. One quarter of Australian vines are to be found here, but a higher proportion of producers than any state. I got to 550 before I stopped counting. The areas are Yarra Valley, Mornington Peninsula, Geelong, Macedon Ranges, The Grampians, Pyrenees, Bendigo, Henty, Heathcote, Goulburn Valley, Upper Goulburn, Nagambie Lakes, Strathbogie Ranges, Rutherglen, Glenrowan, King Valley, Alpine Valleys, Beechworth, Gippsland, Murray Darling/Swan Hill, Port Philip, Central Victoria, and Western Victoria.

Gippsland
Pinot Jones

Phillip Jones not only makes Pinot Noir; he is the ruler, the demagogue, of Australasian Pinot. His wines, bearing the label Bass Phillip, go back-of-shop, under-counter, like smuggled caviar. On a single visit to Melbourne my restaurant expenses were once swollen by AUS$380 (£161) in order to acquire a single bottle of his 1996; it was as concentrated, as sensually aromatic, as beautifully textured a Pinot as I have ever experienced.

His winery is situated some miles from the blink-and-you-miss-it hamlet of Leongatha in Gippsland. The shock is the banality of it all: well-trained vines, decently mature, set in deep banks with plenty of cover crops along the rows. But there's no room for mechanical harvesters between the intimate, hugger-mugger rows. There is not one whit of glamour. It looks like a northern European rural scene; anywhere from Somerset to Denmark. In the distance a cow ruminates, trees sigh in the sharp wind, arable fields lie sullen under bruised clouds. There's surely no need for irrigation in this climate.

Phillip deals with this matter witheringly. He doesn't so much have bags under his eyes as eyes above his bags. His is the well lived-in face of a real human being. "Who needs irrigation?" he declares in a voice like gravel scraping the inside of an iron pot. "No-one in the cooler coastal regions of Australia needs to water their vines."

There is no fifty/fifty with Phillip Jones. His remarks lack ambiguity; they are devoid of superficiality. He is more committed to Pinot Noir than

CLOCKWISE FROM TOP LEFT The sky-line of Melbourne is every bit as dazzling, multi-layered, and rich as Victorian wines.

Perfectly balanced on the barrel head is a mature Victorian red, made in Westburn, 96.5 kilometres (60 miles) east of Melbourne in the Yarra Valley.

The wine list at Kylie Balharrie's and Michael Kennedy's Healesville Hotel in the Yarra Valley is as fresh as the delicious food.

Phillip Jones, Bass Phillip proprietor and winemaker, is more steeped in Pinot Noir – though he drinks the odd Chardonnay – than just about any other Australian.

Moët & Chandon hardly needed much persuading to set up its winery in Coldstream, Victoria, in 1986. Domaine Chandon's vines get the sun, and in the meantime the visitor is obliged with a beautiful outlook.

IN STOCK NOW
- YERINGBERG
- MT MARY
- GEMBROOK
- YERING STATION RESERVES
- DALWHINNIE SHIRAZ
- FELTON ROAD (NZ)
- QUARTZ REEF
- BIRKS WENDOREE

COMING SOON
- ATA RANGI
- MT LANGHI 94

most of those *soi-disant* champions of the grape, the Burgundians. He devotes his life to this island of Pinot, and though he makes wine from other varieties from vineyards elsewhere, Pinot Noir is the focus of his existence and has been for many years, since he gave up the computing business. The only pity is that he is not yet as Biodynamic or organic as he would like to be. Minimal intervention in the vineyard is his policy, but he is not above spraying Bio-Roundup to clear the weeds.

The vines are as moody-looking as Pinot vines can be, and pruned down to two bunches per vine which makes yields very low (one reason why the wine is so expensive). Yet the winery is set in the midst of a shambles. It is surrounded by the detritus of an industrial car boot sale: a mechanical elephants' graveyard of old tanks, a defunct bottling machine, cans, pipes, all sorts of dead metal stuff. The house, where Phillip and his wife Sairung, an opthalmologist, spend some of their time (they have another home a little distance away), reflects this complete devotion to clutter. Phillip is a serial clutterer on a monumental scale. The more self-centred a man, so psychiatrists say, the more untidy his living quarters are likely to be.

When the Pinots appear for tasting, including the legendary 1991, a bottle of Henri Jayer's 1988 Echézeaux is thrown in for comparison. It is spineless compared with the Bass Phillip. No-one makes modern Pinot Noir a more sensual experience than Phillip Jones because he pours his personality into every barrel. He is the grapes' terroir as much as any clod of his nondescript soil. If his new Millennium vintages lack the concentration of his 1990s, as they do, the reason is psychological not geological.

Yarra Valley
Centurians and custodians
If there is one area in Australia to make the heartbeat of any European immigrant grape grower quicken with homesickness, it is here. The Yarra is serene, ordered, undulating; lush without being pompous. It is fine rural architecture of shades of green just an hour from Melbourne by road.

The Valley boasts just about a hundred wine producers. For this taster, the most exciting are Coldstream Hills (Pinot Noir), De Bortoli (Chardonnay), Domaine Chandon (where Moët & Chandon makes Green Point bubbly), Mount Mary (Pinot Noir, Cabernet Sauvignon), Tarrawarra (Chardonnay), Yarra Yarra (Semillon), Yarra Yering (Cabernet), Yering Station (Shiraz), and Yarra Burn (Chardonnay). These estates make wines other than those from the grapes indicated, but these are the ones which have consistently impressed.

It was at James Halliday's Coldstream Hills vineyard that I first tasted Australian Pinot Noir berries, off the vine, as succulent as those from Mendocino in California. The vineyard has since been sold to Southcorp, but its ex-proprietor continues his involvement as consultant.

It was at Yarra Burn's so-called Bastard Hill that one appreciated its name. The vineyard is preposterously, insanely steep. It also faces south (away from the sun). Clearly, whoever laid it out was totally mad. The man who did this, or who certainly played a major part in choosing such a precipitous vineyard, is viticulturalist Ray Guerin. Ray lives on the Yarra Burn property of which Bastard Hill is a part and he has the greenest of green fingers, as evidenced by the profusion of flowers and shrubs. Bastard Hill Chardonnay, now made by ex-cheesemaker, ex-professional chef Steve Flamsteed, can be extraordinary: more-than-a-little burgundian with a touch of the exotic.

Geelong
Windy city
I've never been in Geelong and not felt a stiff breeze. The dockside city itself (it calls itself a city not a town, and with 200,000 citizens, why not?) seems indifferent to the three dozen wine producers the area can muster. The winds of change which revived the vineyards' fortunes here did not occur until recently, so this was yet another frontier spot. The most prominent producers only got going in the 1970s, 1980s, and later. But there are stars and would-be stars. Bannockburn has its Pinot Noir, Bellarine its Chardonnay, By Farr a Viognier so focussed I even bought two cases myself (and for a wine writer to put his hand in his pocket is a rare and lovely event), Jindalee a brash but scrumptious Chardonnay, Provenance a remarkable Shiraz, and Scotchmans Hill a tight Shiraz, an impressive Pinot Noir, and a toothsome Chardonnay.

Provenance and Shadowfax are two of the newer boys. The Shadowfax winery, a building made of rusting steel sheets (a stylistic trick borrowed from the design of Melbourne's Centre for Contemporary Arts), easily justifies being named after Gandalf's horse in the *Lord of the Rings*. The building is a flight of fancy and the flight of wines fanciful and ambitious. "Our focus is Shiraz," says winemaker Matt Harrop. "I worked in Italy for a vintage and I liked the lack of respect they showed their whites." A very rich Sauvignon Blanc and an abundantly fruity Chardonnay demonstrate that he cares more than he knows.

Shadowfax reds are not so disrespectful, more insular. The Pinot Noirs are sweet. A Sangiovese/Merlot has gloomy tannins. The more impressive Shirazes simper. This is a young winery, established in 1997, and it has a little way to go yet. Matt's wines will increase in concentration and maturity as he does. He needs to get out and raise hell a bit and then the wines will really be something.

Bannockburn once had Gary Farr as its winemaker. Now he has his own show, By Farr. His liquids manifest all of their maker's combative intelligence and forthrightness, not just in that brilliant By Farr Viognier, but in some of his old Bannockburn Pinot Noirs.

Robin Brockett, chief winemaker and viticulturalist at Scotchmans Hill, also makes the wines for Bellarine Estate. He is passionate on the subject of screwcaps. "I was invited to Portugal," he says, "to visit the cork forests and see cork being made. It's put me off cork forever. They can't

cure cork taint no matter what they do. I was shocked by how much money the government gives them not for research but for advertising. When I came back from Portugal I changed my cork supplier and decided we had to think seriously about screwcaps." Robin also makes, and scores, good points with his wines, one of the the most pertinent being the Swan Bay Pinot Noir.

Scotchmans Hill is owned by the Brownes, David and Vivienne, who like taking visitors to the pub, The Ol' Duke in Portarlington. "I would cook," says Vivienne, her bright blonde hair shimmering like a nimbus, "but I did it for twenty-five years and now I've discovered business which is so absorbing that I've no time to prepare food." Before son Michael came of age and joined the business, Vivienne helped stockbroker David run the Scotchmans Hill office.

A little history lesson

The drive to Jindalee may remind the British visitor of a trip to Wolverhampton in early winter. But that's this part of Victoria for you: bristling with British manners and British skies and stiff-upper lips worn like moustaches. "By 1870 it was the largest wine region in Victoria," says my chauffeur, Provenance's Scott Ireland. "Then phylloxera came and wiped out most of it. The oldest vines in the region were planted in Jindalee's Idyll vineyard in 1966."

It was the Idyll estate that in 1998 was purchased by two brothers, David and Vince Littore, from Mildura (up in the hot north of the state where grapes grow abundantly ripe in front of your eyes), and turned in to Jindalee. The fruit is shipped down, as juice, in refrigerated trucks to the Geelong winery, where it becomes millions of bottles of value-for-money red wines of the sort which makes the French hopping mad. By judicious stirring of the lees with the Chardonnays, the lip-smackin'est wine here, and a gentle twenty per cent malolactic second fermentation, Scott, when he was in charge, fashioned a range of unpretentious wines of charm and concentration. Andrew Byers is now winemaker.

Scott's own range of wines, Provenance, reflects more his own passionate personality. The Pinot Noir, drunk three hours after decanting with some gamey sausages, enters into a very happy food and wine marriage. Scott also makes, at the same address, the wines for Richard and Pamela Austin at Austin's Barrabool, but these wines are yet to pass this taster's lips.

Good Mornington Peninsula
Cool climate? Or just cool winemakers?

The ferry ride from Queenscliff in Geelong to Sorrento in the Mornington is almost as straightforward and uneventful as the one between Dover and Calais. The ferries cross the huge Port Phillip bay, a natural harbour, as it describes a circle with the ocean at the bottom, Melbourne at the top.

At Dromana Estate the winemaking is done by Rollo Crittenden who took over from father Garry (who now runs Crittenden at Dromana Wines). Dromana Estate, which got itself listed on the London Alternative Investment Market as well as on the Aussie Stock Exchange (and declared a loss of AUS$470,000/£200,000 for 2004/05), had, under Garry, created a reputation for making interesting wines from Italian varieties such as Arneis, Barbera, Sangiovese, and Nebbiolo. There must be at least seventy-five producers in the Mornington and in its day none was more adventurous than this one.

At the Lindenderry Hotel, which is surrounded by Red Hill Vineyards, several local winemakers stand the author dinner with a range of wines – and stories. Nat White's Main Ridge Estate Chardonnay stands out, as does his anecdote about visiting Berry Bros & Rudd in St James's in London in the early 1980s and admitting he made wine and that perhaps BBR might look at importing some. "But… you're Australian!" spluttered the three-piece-suited assistant and showed him the door. Whether they still sport waistcoats at this wine merchant I know not, but I do know the staff would not be so cavalier with Aussie visitors today.

Day and night

Stoniers is a Mornington Peninsula vineyard owned by Brian Croser's Petaluma group, which itself has been gobbled up by the Lion-Nathan conglomerate. It makes a brave sparkling wine, Chardonnay, and Pinot Noirs. The theme is understatement.

In barrel, the Chardonnays and Pinot Noirs, before going into a final blend, are impressive. The barrel cellar is the place where the truly creative winemaker, in this case Geraldine McFaul, can shine. It is also evident from the zestiness of the wine that though the Mornington may show little difference between its night time and day time temperatures, it is a cool climate area.

The Stonier winery exudes efficiency and neatness. Just like the wines. By contrast, by huge, vivid contrast, T'Gallant is the antithesis of neatness and control. Yet it turns out the most remarkable Pinot Gris in Australia. Kathleen Quealy, who runs the place with husband Kevin McCarthy, once remarked to me, many years ago, that she wouldn't mind at all if some big, rich company came along and made her an offer she couldn't refuse. In April 2003, the big, rich company did come along and it was called Beringer Blass.

Luckily, for Beringer Blass and Pinot Gris lovers, Kathleen and Kevin are still involved. They are two of the most entertaining winemakers, parents, café operators, and talkers on the peninsula. T'Gallant stands for wine as artistry, as reflected in their imaginative, risk-taking label designs. And the liquids inside the bottles? The Tribute Pinot Gris, with its subtle apricot richness and soft acidity, lingers like a welcome guest. It is a remarkable wine, but then all T'Gallant's various Pinot Gris are interesting; the same can be said for a vibrant, sensual, spicy Sangiovese.

Kathleen has strong views about oak and its prevalence in Australia. "It's all bullshit," she exclaims. "You mean the lynchpin of a wine and its winery must be French oak? Bullshit! Wine should speak without oak cluttering things up. And what about the economics? For the cost of a new barrel I can prune more than an acre of my vineyard. Oak is an Australian disease. The economics speak for themselves."

One wonders, now it is owned by Beringer Blass with its fondness for oak, if T'Gallant will change its tune. Ms Quealy, however, is not a woman who sings from anyone else's songsheet.

LEFT The T'Gallant winery, run by Kathleen Quealy and Kevin McCarthy, goes in for deliciously quirky wine sporting deliciously quirky labels.

RIGHT The Ritchies, brother David and sister Rosalind, of the Delatite winery, produce wines as fluently forthright as they are from a wide variety of grapes.

Upper Goulburn

Getting a load of Buller

The Upper Goulburn has fewer than twenty producers, one of which is among the most compelling in Australia: Delatite. The Delatite winery, run by Rosalind Ritchie and brother David, is only fifteen minutes' drive from Victoria's St Moritz, the ski slopes of Mount Buller. There is not just a lot to see here, and fascinating wines to taste, there is a lot to talk about.

Will the estate, as it wants to do, go Biodynamic and follow the viticultural precepts of Rudolf Steiner? Since David's children attend a Steiner infants school he obviously has an interest in the man and his ideas. Biodynamism denies any role for pesticides, herbicides, fungicides, and artificial fertilizers, insists that a vineyard must be part of a polyculture, relies on phases of the moon and the changing seasons, and is designed to make fruit wholly a part of nature and not an agricultural product grown in an outdoor factory.

And what wines come from this scenic estate! Unique, handsome, textured, individual, couth, complex, caressing yet characterful, both reds and whites are a treat – though deliciously atypical of Australian vinous liquids. Demelza, a 100 per cent Pinot Noir bubbly, displays elegance and finesse. The unwooded Chardonnay is pure fruit. Sauvignon Blanc offers dry mango and gooseberry. A Pinot Gris is vivacious yet controlled. A Gewurztraminer has the usual lychee with an added hint of lime. The Riesling is concentrated and fine.

If the whites are interesting (to put it limply), then the Delatite reds are equally potently provocative. The Malbec may be sappy, and light on essential tannins, but a Cabernet Sauvignon, a Shiraz, and a Devil's River Cabernet had this taster gasping for superlatives as ratings of 18 points

out of 20 were bestowed. These were outstanding cool climate wines of friendly intensity and individuality – just like the Ritchies brother and sister. The reds had that northern Italian feel of whiplash tannicity and alpine freshness.

Pyrenees and Grampians
Neighbours in name only

David and Jenny Jones run Dalwhinnie Estate. It is the most beautifully situated and deliciously undulating of the Pyrenees vineyards, and at nearly 600 metres (1969 feet) above sea level, the highest. It overlooks the Moonambel Valley. That the soul of a winemaker is more important than the soil of the vineyard is proven as one studies the landscape.

For, cheek by jowl with Dalwhinnie is the much larger vineyard of Taltarni, once described by a British wine hack as the most beautifully laid-out in the world. But whereas Taltarni is happy to grow seven or eight tons of grapes to a hectare, David and Jenny are more conservative and take around three to four tons from each hectare. The vineyards look different as well. Taltarni is irrigated. Dalwhinnie is all dryland fruit and the water from the dams is used in the winery, not on the vines. Even with seven years of drought, not a drop of irrigated water is permitted to touch the vines. David, in fact, is one of those rare perfectionists who is not a neurotic. He will not make wine from under-age vines, which is why he has sold the Shiraz from his newer vines to Scotchmans Hill. "I can really taste the resin from the stems of young vines. I won't make wine from young vines. They have to be at least eight years old minimum before I'll make wine from them."

Dalwhinnie was started by David's dad, Ewan, in October 1973. And Ewan's parents gave him a good start in life. His mother's family owned a gold mine. His father was a successful Ballarat builder (the best profession to practice in a boom town and even today, nearly eight decades later, there are 300 builders in Ballarat each with plenty of work). Ewan married into a family of grocers when he wed Betty Ritchie. And it was the Ritchies who came from the village of Dalwhinnie in Scotland.

Ewan became an architect in Ballarat but wanted a vineyard on the side and so he purchased the scrub, complete with the pathetic mechanical remains of old gold mines from the previous century, and began to conceive of a vineyard. David Hohnen designed the original vineyard in 1976 when he worked at the neighbouring Taltarni Estate. David has since gone on to his own fame and fortune at Cape Mentelle in Western Australia and Cloudy Bay in Marlborough in New Zealand. Dalwhinnie vines are now looked after by Colin Jardine. The wines are made by David himself.

He is moving the vines to becoming wholly organic. "We do spray some Bio-Roundup against the weeds because it's too expensive to hoe them out. But once I acquire that AUS$15,000 (£6,400) mechanical hoeing machine then it's goodbye to chemicals."

He doesn't even need to spray a fungicide against botrytis...? "Never. Not in the Pyrenees. We don't get any sort of rot up here."

For David, the health of his vines is like the health of his children. "At the end of the day a vine will tell you what it can do and what it can't. If you have healthy vines – and you can apply the same analogy to human beings – then if they're fit they're less likely to come down with things."

On a tour of the thirty-three hectares of vines, stepping over the snakes, avoiding the kangaroo poo, returning the koalas' greetings and the cockatoo's goodbyes, David gestures at the flowers on the gum trees and the floribundance of nuts and fruit flowers on the orchard trees. He exults in the wild beauty of this place. The drinker exults in the wild beauty of Dalwhinnie Chardonnays, Cabernet Sauvignons, Shirazes, and if he can find them, the wondrous Pinot Noirs which even Phillip Jones at Bass Phillip would not scorn to admire.

Returning to the fold

Blue Pyrenees, once called Château Rémy after its Cognac owners, changed its name after Rainbow Warrior was blown up.

Now in Aussie hands, in days gone by it was the very model of the post-war French approach to viticulture and one reason perhaps why it did not perform as well as it should. Every fourteen days the 220 hectares were sprayed with sulphur, a wetting agent, fungicides, zinc, anti-powdery mildew, anti-downy mildew, and anti-botrytis agents (with another botrytis spray to help fruit set). In the fashion of Bordeaux properties there were rose bushes growing at the head of certain vine rows. Were the flowers there to catch the early onset of certain vine diseases so preventative action could be taken? Vineyard manager, Andre des Barres, a Kiwi with an impressive Asterix-style moustache, who embraces a wholly different mode of viticulture, laughs and shakes his head: "Roses are useful only if you have an argument with the wife. You can't buy flowers anywhere round here."

Trevor Mast at Mount Langi Ghiran in the Grampians is just the sort of man to bring his wife flowers. He looks disconcertingly like the romantic novelist Sebastian Faulks. Langi Ghiran has turned out, under the two-decades-plus stewardship of Mr Mast, some of Australia's most highly regarded Shirazes as well as Cabernets, Rieslings, and a gritty Pinot Gris which treads a perfect middle ground between the apricotty Alsatian approach and the drier, more neurotic Italian style.

Viv-acity

No visit to Victoria can be accomplished without seeing Viv Thomson of Best's Wines in the Grampians. This is one of those family estates where the nature of the family permeates everything it does – from the vineyard fruit to the food on the table, from the piano in the living room to the two dogs and one cat which manage amicably to live together. It is an historic estate, one of Australia's oldest. It traces its lineage back to 1866. Riesling,

LEFT-HAND PAGE

TOP LEFT Not everything in Adelaide is state-of-the-art and, with regard to the Glenelg tram, the city is all the more charming for it.

TOP CENTRE You can pick up fruit to-die-for in Adelaide's popular and hugely diverse food market.

TOP RIGHT The old lady who gave the state of Victoria its name (and, so it is said, its inhabitants their regal demeanour).

BELOW The Barossa is home to some of Australia's most intense red wines – from vineyards heavily in debt to the interventions of skilled viticulturalists.

RIGHT-HAND PAGE

TOP A plane view of a plain of Victorian vineyards.

CENTRE The bigger cities in Australia – Melbourne, Sydney, Perth, Brisbane, Adelaide – are never far from water and trees.

BELOW Dog Lucky, Ewan Jones, and a Melhuselah (eight bottles all in one) of dad David's glorious Dalwhinnie red wine.

AUSTRALIA

57

Chardonnay, Pinot Noir, Cabernet, Merlot, and Shiraz – there is not a dull wine in the bunch, though most impressive are the Swan Hill Shiraz, the Great Western Shiraz, and a Great Western Cabernet. The Rieslings and the Pinots can, though, take a few years to come good. An astonishingly virile twenty-six-year-old Best's Riesling, which shows a marvellous toffee and lemon sherbet fruitiness, was made by Trevor Mast when he cut his teeth here. An eleven-year-old Pinot Noir displays a chocolate edge and an unusual damson jamminess, yet dryness.

Boutique Beechworth

There are around a dozen producers in this tiny area, but one giant: Giaconda. Giaconda, in Beechworth Victoria, is a cult-status vineyard run by Rick Kinzbrunner. The Chardonnay can be tremendous and tremendously expensive, but you can find Melbourne restaurateurs ready to part with a bottle for ready cash. Not all its wines, however, are so pungent and awesome.

Tasting a Giaconda Aeoloia Roussanne, made from the Rhône white grape, burned the back of the throat with its 13.6% ABV.

Goulburn Valley and Nagambie
Mushroom wines

McPherson's, in the Goulburn Valley, is one of those mushroom success stories of the Aussie wine industry like Jindalee and Yellow Tail. Launched in 1993, it turns out over 1,000,000 cases of wine a year, mainly from fruit sent down from the Murray-Darling region up north. It is the fifth largest

LEFT Tahbilk Estate in the Goulburn Valley can boast some of the world's oldest productive Shiraz vines (including one like this, 1860 on its birth certificate, said to be the most antique of all).

RIGHT Don Lewis, Mitchelton's winemaker, turns out wines as characterful, yet soft at heart, as he is.

Aussie brand in the USA. McPherson's was once the house Aussie Shiraz in the Novotel chain in France. Guido Vazzoler, the winemaker, makes decently commercial offerings, though the more expensive Reserve range shows greater individuality and bite.

A beautiful place to make love
Tahbilk Estate in the Goulburn used to be called Château Tahbilk, but such titular pretensions are now uncool and owner Alister Purbrick has seen sense and ditched the château bit (*tahbilk*, much more amusingly, is allegedly Aborigine for "beautiful place to make love").

"Apart from getting into the third millennium, and being proudly Australian," explains Alister, "the French connotation was out of date. Besides, EU regulations have outlawed it."

The wines here are, apart from the young Marsannes, old-fashioned and with challenging acidic structures. There is good cellaring potential in those Marsannes (and the Rieslings), but the reds can be uncompromisingly sere and arthritic, slow-moving, big, thick, alcoholic, concentrated wines of little subtlety. Tradition runs through the fruit, which is dry and autumnal, in contrast to the general run of Aussie reds which are summery and fruity. These are uncouth, brusque wines when young with a shaggy dog unsociability. The reds are potent, individual, proud, uncompromising – they have an intensely parochial, aristocratic, craggy integrity, true to themselves. You can love them as much as you can loathe them. To taste these red wines at the estate is to consume history in its own gloriously musty museum, and that mustiness, in spirit, infuses the wines. One steps back in time when tasting here, both in terms of spirit of place as in liquid on palate. Of course the prices are aristocratic. Indeed, AUS$120 (£51) a bottle for a decently mature 1860s Vines Shiraz is verging on the imperial.

At Mitchelton, a winery beautifully situated on the Goulburn River, the wines do not challenge the pocket so outrageously but they do challenge the palate. Winemaker Don Lewis can take the privileged visitor through a most impressive line-up of wines. How does he manage to combine such a wily commercial sense of what the market wants with such individuality and genuine complexity of fruit? The bottom end Thomas Mitchelton whites and reds are all sound and balanced, the Preece wines purposeful and shapely, and the top end stuff in a class, for the money, by itself. The two most stunning wines, lithe and sensuous, are the Mitchelton Crescent Shiraz/Mourvedre/Grenache and Mitchelton Print Shiraz, surely one of the sauciest in all of Australia.

On the walk to the car which will return this visitor to Melbourne, it is impossible to ignore the abundance of magpies on the lawn. They caper and carol in an exuberant display of fervour.

"Our population of magpies," says Don, "has increased ten-fold since we cut out spraying the vines."

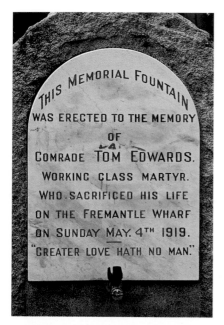

THIS MEMORIAL FOUNTAIN
WAS ERECTED TO THE MEMORY
OF
COMRADE TOM EDWARDS.
WORKING CLASS MARTYR.
WHO SACRIFICED HIS LIFE
ON THE FREMANTLE WHARF
ON SUNDAY MAY. 4TH 1919.
"GREATER LOVE HATH NO MAN."

LEFT-HAND PAGE

TOP LEFT Freemantle, just below
Perth in Western Australia, was not
always as peaceful as it is now. Tom
Edwards died when the local
stevedores clashed with police just
after WWI.

TOP RIGHT A sparrowhawk near
vines is a good indication of a
pesticide-free environment. This is
because there is no disruption to the
faunal food chain, from insect to bird
to larger winged predator.

BELOW The banks of the mighty
Murray River, the aqueous artery of
South Australia (though it touches
Victoria and New South Wales too).

RIGHT-HAND PAGE

RIGHT Everything grows tall in
Australia, whatever your perspective
(as here, looking across from the
Royal Botanical Gardens at Sydney).

TOP The shed where Ned Kelly was finally nabbed in June 1880, in Glenrowan, Victoria.

BELOW LEFT Len Evans, doyen of Australian wine, giant of the unique Australian wine show scene, relaxes in his back garden. "I'm writing a novel," he told me, "about a man who's searching for the perfect wine."

BELOW RIGHT Though several decades old, this bottle of Tahbilk Riesling contained liquid to thrill the eye, fully engage the nose, and stun the palate.

TOP Machines can prune vines, they can pick grapes, they can bottle the wine. What they can never do is appreciate the liquid.

BELOW LEFT Peter Forrestal, wine judge, does it with food at the Sydney International Wine Competition. To face kangaroo pie (just after breakfast) along with thirty-eight Shirazes is, let me tell you, tough going.

BELOW RIGHT Leo Buring has been in the Barossa since 1931. The Leonay vineyard is in New South Wales, however, and it is but a memory, for it is now part of the landscaped township of Leonay (on the Nepean River, at the foot of the Blue Mountains).

Australia's winemakers

SOUTH AUSTRALIA
CLARE VALLEY
GROSSET
King Street, Auburn,
South Australia 5451
Tel: 8 8849 2175. Fax: 8 8849 2292
info@grosset.com.au. www.grosset.com.au
Winemaker: Jeffrey Grosset

KNAPPSTEIN
2 Pioneer Avenue, Clare, SA 5453
Tel: 8 8842 2600. Fax: 8 8842 3831
cellardoor@knappsteinwines.com.au
www.knappsteinwines.com.au
Winemaker: Andrew Hardy

LEASINGHAM
7 Dominic Street, Clare,
South Australia 5453
Tel: 8 8842 2555. Fax: 8 8842 3293
www.leasingham-wines.com.au
Winemaker: Kerri Thompson

MOUNT HORROCKS
Curling Street, Auburn,
South Australia 5451
Tel: 8 849 2243. Fax: 8 8849 2243
www.mounthorrocks.com
Winemakers: Stephanie Toole and
Jeffrey Grosset

SKILLOGALEE
Off Hughes Park Road, Sevenhill via
Clare, SA 5453. Tel: 8 8843 4311
Fax: 8 8843 4343. skilly@chariot.net.au
www.skillogalee.com.au
Winemaker: Daniel & Dave Palmer

WENDOUREE
Wendouree Road, Clare,
South Australia 5453
Tel: 8 8843 4395
Winemaker: Tony Brady

BAROSSA
BAROSSA VALLEY ESTATE
Seppeltsfield Road, Marananga, SA 5117
Tel: 8 8562 3599. Fax: 8 8562 4255
bve@chariot.net.au. www.bve.com.au
Winemaker: Fiona Donald

BASEDOW
161-5 Murray Street, Tanunda, SA 5352
Tel: 8 8563 3666. Fax: 8 8563 3597
www.basedow.com.au
Winemaker: Craig Stansborough

BETHANY
Bethany Road, Bethany via Tanunda,
SA 5352. Tel: 8 8563 2086. Fax: 8 8563 0046
bethany@bethany.com.au
www.bethany.com.au
Winemakers: Geoff Schrapel, Robert
Schrapel

CHARLES MELTON
Krondorf Road, Tanunda, SA 5352
Tel: 8 8563 3606. Fax: 8 8563 3422
cmw@charlesmeltonwines.com.au
www.charlesmeltonwines.com.au
Winemaker: Charlie Melton

GLAETZER
34 Barossa Valley Way, Tanunda, SA 5352.
Tel: 8 8563 0288. Fax: 8 8563 0218
www.glaetzer.com
Winemakers: Colin Glaetzer, Ben Glaetzer

GRANT BURGE
Barossa Valley Way, Jacobs Creek,
Tanunda, SA 5352
Tel: 8 8563 3700. Fax: 8 8563 2807
admin@grantburgewines.com.au
www.grantburgewines.com.au
Winemaker: Grant Burge

LEO BURING
Tanunda Road, Nurioopta, SA 5355
Tel: 8 8560 9408
www.leoburing.com.au
Winemaker: Geoff Henriks

ORLANDO
Barossa Valley Way, Rowland Flat,
SA 5352. Tel: 8 8521 3111
Fax: 8 8521 3100. www.jacobscreek.com
Winemaker: Phil Laffer

PENFOLDS
Penfolds, Southcorp Limited,
78 Penfolds Road, P.O. Box 96, Magill,
South Australia 5072
Tel: 8 8301 5400. Fax: 8 8301 5544
www.southcorp.com.au
Chief winemaker: Peter Gago

PETER LEHMANN
Para Road, Tanunda, SA 5352
Tel: 8 8563 2500. Fax: 8 8563 3402
www.peterlehmannwines.com
Winemakers: Peter Lehmann, Andrew
Wigan, Peter Scholz, Leonie Lange

ROCKFORD
Krondorf Road, Tanunda, SA 5352
Tel: 8 8563 2720. Fax: 8 8563 3787
info@rockfordwines.com.au
Winemakers: Robert O'Callaghan,
Chris Ringland

SALTRAM
Nurioopta-Angaston Road,
Angaston, SA 5353
Tel: 8 8564 3355. Fax: 8 8564 3384
cellardoor@saltramestate.com.au
www.saltramestate.com.au
Winemaker: Nigel Dolan

ST HALLETT
St Hallett's Road, Tanunda, SA 5352
Tel: 8 8563 7000. Fax: 8 8563 7001
sthallett@sthallett.com.au
www.sthallett.com.au
Winemakers: Staurt Blackwell, Neil
Doddridge, Cathy Spratt

TORBRECK
Roennfeldt Road, Maranga, South
Australia. P.O. Box 583, Tanunda SA 5352
Tel: 8 8562 4155. Fax: 8 8562 4195
info@torbreck.com. www.torbreck.com
Founder winemaker: David Powell
Winemaker: Dan Standish

WOLF BLASS
Bilyara Vineyards, Sturt Highway,
Nuriootpa, SA 5355. Tel: 8 8562 1955
Fax: 8 8562 2156. www.wolfblass.com.au
Winemakers: John Glaetzer (red), Wendy
Stuckey (white)

YALUMBA
Angaston-Eden Valley Road,
Angaston, SA 5353
Tel: 8 8561 3200. Fax: 8 8561 3393
info@yalumba.com. www.yalumba.com
Winemaker: Simon Adams

MCLAREN VALE
ADELAIDE HILLS
Starve Dog Lane from The Lane Wines
Ravenswood Lane, Hahndorf, SA 5245
Tel: 8 8388 1250
Winemakers: John Edwards, Marty Edwards

CORIOLE
Chaffeys Road, McLaren Vale,
South Australia 5171
Tel: 8 8323 8305. Fax: 8 8323 9136
contact@coriole.com. www.coriole.com
Winemaker: Grant Harrison

D'ARENBURG
Osborn Road, McLaren Vale,
South Australia 5171
Tel: 8 8323 8206. Fax: 8 8323 8423
winery@darenberg.com.au
www.darenberg.com.au
Winemaker: Chester Osborn

HARDY'S CHATEAU REYNELLA
Reynell Rd, Reynella, SA 5161
Tel: 8 8392 2222. Fax: 8 8392 2154
corporale@hardywines.com.au
www.hardywines.com.au
Winemakers: Peter Dawson, Stephen
Pannell, Tom Newton, Ed Carr

KANGARILLA ROAD WINERY
Kangarilla & Hamilton's Road, McLaren
Vale, South Australia 5171
Tel: 8 8383 0533. Fax: 8 8383 0044
kangarillaroad@bigpond.com
www.kangarillaroad.com.au
Winemaker: Kevin O'Brien

SERAFINO WINES
Kangarilla Road, McLaren Vale, South
Australia 5171
Tel: 8 8323 0157. Fax: 8 8323 0158
serafinowines@mclarensonthelake.com.au
www.mclarensonthelake.com.au
Winemaker: Scott Rawlinson

WIRRA WIRRA
McMurtie Road, McLaren Vale,
South Australia, 5171
Tel: 8 8323 8414. Fax: 8 8323 8596
info@wirra.com.au. www.wirra.com.au
Winemaker: Ben Riggs

COONAWARRA
BALNAVES
Main Road, Coonawarra, Southy Australia
Tel: 8 8737 2946. Fax: 8 8737 2945
kirsty.balnaves@balnaves.com.au
www.balnaves.com.au
Winemaker: Peter Bissell

HOLLICK
Riddoch Highway, Coonawarra, SA 5263
Tel: 8 8737 2318. Fax: 8 8737 2952
admin@hollick.com. www.hollick.com
Winemaker: Ian Hollick

JAMIESONS RUN
Penola-Naracoote Road, Coonawarra, SA
5263. Tel: 8 8736 3380. Fax: 8 9736 3071
cellardoor@jamiesonsrun.com.au
www.jamiesonsrun.com.au
Winemaker: Andrew Hales

KATNOOK ESTATE
Riddoch Hiughway, Coonawarra, South
Australia 5263. Tel: 8 8737 2394
Fax: 8 8737 2397. katnook@wingara.com.au
www.katnookestate.com.au
Winemaker: Wayne Stehbens

PENLEY ESTATE
McLeans Rd, Coonamwarra, SA 5263
Tel: 8 8736 3211. Fax: 8 8736 3124
www.penley.com.au. Winemaker: Kym Tolley

RYMILL
Riddoch Run Vineyards, Coonawarra, SA
5263. Tel: 8 8736 5001. Fax: 8 8736 5040
winery@rymill.com.au. www.rymill.com.au
Winemakers: John Innes, Clémence
Haselgrove

WYNNS COONAWARRA ESTATE
Memorial Drive, Coonawarra, SA 5263
Tel: 8 8736 2225. Fax: 8 8736 2228
www.wynns.com.au
Winemaker: Sue Hodder

NEW SOUTH WALES
ORANGE
BLOODWOOD WINES
4 Griffin Road, Orange, New South Wales
2800. Tel: 2 6362 5631. Fax: 2 6361 1173
BigMen@bloodwood.com.au
www.bloodwood.com.au
Winemaker: Stephen Doyle

LOWER HUNTER VALLEY

ALLANDALE
Lovedale Rd, Lovedale, NSW 2320
Tel: 2 4990 4526. Fax: 2 4990 1714
wines@allandalewinery.com.au
www.allandalewinery.com.au
Winemaker: Bill Sneddon

BROKENWOOD
McDonalds Road, Pokolobin, New South
Wales 2320.Tel: 2 4998 7559
Fax: 2 4998 7893. sales@brokenwood.com.au
www.brokenwood.com.au
Winemaker: Iain Riggs

MCWILLIAMS MOUNT PLEASANT
Marrowbone Rd, Pokolbin, NSW 2320
Tel: 2 4998 7505. Fax: 2 4998 7761
www.mcwilliams.com.au
Winemaker: Phillip Ryan

MEEREA PARK
Lot 3, Palmers Lane, Pokolbin, NSW 2320
Tel: 2 4998 7474. www.meereapark.com.au
Winemaker: Rhys Eather

PENDARVES ESTATE
110 Old North Rd, Belford, NSW 2335
Tel: 2 6574 7222. www.winedoctor.info
Winemaker: Dr Phillip Norrie

THE ROTHBURY ESTATE
Broke Rd, Pokolbin, NSW 2321
Tel: 2 4998 7363. Winemaker: Mike DeGaris

SCARBOROUGH WINE COMPANY
Gillards Road, Pokolobin, New South
Wales 2320
Tel: 2 4998 7563. Fax: 2 4998 7786
sales@scarboroughwine.com.au
www.scarboroughwine.com.au
Winemaker: Ian Scarborough

TYRRELL'S, BROKE ROAD
Pokolbin, New South Wales 2320
Tel: 2 4993 7000. Fax: 2 4993 7059
info@tyrrells.com.au. www.tyrrells.com.au
Winemaker: Mark Richardson

WYNDHAM ESTATE
700 Dalwood Road, Dalwood, New South
Wales 2335. www.wyndhamestate.com.au
Chief Winemaker: Brett McKinnon

UPPER HUNTER VALLEY

ROSEMOUNT ESTATE
Rosemount Rd, Denman, NSW 2328
Tel: 2 6547 2556. www.rosemountestate.com
Winemakers: Charles Whish, Matt Koch,
Briony Hoare

MUDGEE

ANDREW HARRIS VINEYARDS
Sydney Road, PO Box 1025, Mudgee, New
South Wales 2850
Tel: 2 6373 1213. Fax: 2 6373 1296
marketing@andrewharris.com.au
www.andrewharris.com.au
Winemaker: Frank Newman

HUNTINGTON ESTATE
Cassilis Road, Mudgee, New Souyth
Wales 2850
Tel: 2 6373 3825. Fax: 2 6373 3730
info@huntingtonestate.com.au
www.huntingtonestate.com.au
Winemaker: Susan Roberts

QUEENSLAND

SOUTH BURNETT

BARAMBAH RIDGE
79 Goschnicks Road, Redgate via Murgon,
Queensland 4605
Tel: 7 4168 4766. Fax: 7 4168 4770
info@barambahridge.com.au
www.barambahridge.com.au
Winemaker: Stuart Pierce

CAPTAIN'S PADDOCK
PO Box 500, 18 Millars Road, Kingaroy,
Queensland 4610
Tel: 7 4162 4534. Fax: 7 4162 4502
wine@captainspaddock.com.au
www.captainspaddock.com.au
Winemakers: Ross Whiteford for Maryanne
& Peter Pidcock

CLOVELY ESTATE
Steinhardts Road, Moffatdale,
Queensland 4605.
Tel: 7 4168 4788. Fax: 7 4168 4783
cellardoor@clovely.com.au
www. clovely.com.au
Winemakers: Luke Fitzpatrick, David Lowe

CRANE
Hayden's Road, Booie via Kingaroy,
Queensland 4610
Tel: 7 4162 7647. Fax: 7 4162 8381
info@cranewines.com.au
www.cranewines.com.au
Winemaker: John Crane

ROBERT CHANNON
Bradley Lane, Stanthorpe, Queensland
4380.Tel: 7 4683 3260. Fax: 7 4683 3109
info@robertchannonwines.com
www.robertchannonwines.com
Winemaker: Mark Ravenscroft

SIRROMET
850–938 Mount Cotton Road, Mount
Cotton, Queensland 4165
Tel: 7 3206 2999. Fax: 7 3206 0900
wines@sirromet.com. www.sirromet.com
Winemakers: Alain Rousseau, Adam
Chapman

STUART RANGE ESTATES
P.O.Box 213, 67 William Street, Kingaroy,
Queensland 4610.Tel: 7 4162 3711
Fax: 7 4162 4811. info@srewines.com.au
www.stuartrange.com.au
Winemaker: Ross Whiteford

SYMPHONY HILL
2017 Eukey Road, Ballandean,
Queensland 4382. Tel: 7 4684 1399
info@symphonyhill.com.au
www.symphonyhill.com.au
Winemaker: Blair Duncan

WESTERN AUSTRALIA
GREAT SOUTHERN
ALKOOMI
Wingeballup Road, Frankland, WA 6396
Tel: 8 9855 2229. Fax: 8 9855 2284
info@alkoomiwines.com.au
www.alkoomiwines.com.au
Winemakers: Michael Sandiford,
Merv Lange

FRANKLAND ESTATE
Frankland Road, Frankland, WA 6396
Tel: 8 9855 1544. Fax: 8 9855 1549
info@franklandestate.com.au
www.franklandestate.com.au
Winemakers: Barrie Smith, Judy Cullam

HOWARD PARK
Scotsdale Road, Denmark, WEA6333
Tel: 8 9848 2345. Fax: 8 9848 2064
denmark@hpw.com.au
www.howardparkwines.com.au
Winemakers: John Wade, Michael Kerrigan

PLANTAGENET
Albany Highway, Mount Barker, WA6324
Tel: 8 9851 2150
sales@plantagenetwines.com
www.plantagenetwines.com
Winemaker: Gavin Berry

MARGARET RIVER

CAPE MENTELLE
Cape Mentelle, Off Wallcliffe Road,
Margaret River, Western Australia 6285
Tel: 8 9757 3266. Fax: 8 9757 3233
info@capementelle.com.au
www.capementelle.com.au
Winemaker: John Durham

CULLEN
Caves Roiad, Cowaramup, Western
Australia 6284
Tel: 8 9755 5277. Fax: 8 9755 5550
enquiries@cullenwines.com.au
www.cullenwines.com.au
Winemaker: Vanya Cullen

LEEUWIN ESTATE
Stevens Roiad, Margaret River, Western
Australia 6285. Tel: 8 9430 4099
Fax: 8 9430 5687. www.leeuwinestate.com.au
Winemaker: Bob Cartwright

MOSS WOOD
Metricup Road, Wilyabrup, WA 6280
Tel: 8 9755 6266. Fax: 8 9755 6303
mosswood@mosswood.com.au
www.mosswood.com.au
Winemaker: Keith Mugford

PIERRO
Caves Road, Wilyabrup via Cowaramup
WA 6284. Tel: 8 9755 6220. Fax: 8 9755 6308
pierro@iinet.net.au. www.pierro.com.au
Winemaker: Michael Peterkin

VASSE FELIX,
Caves Road/Harmans Road South,
Wilyabrup, WA 6284. Tel: 8 9756 5000
info@vassefelix.com.au
www.vassefelix.com.au
Winemaker: Clive Otto

GEOGRAPHE
CAPEL VALE
Lot 5, Stirling Estate, Mallokup Road,
Capel, WA 6271. Tel: 8 9727 1986
Winemakers: Kristen Jonsson, Bob Bowen

TASMANIA
JANSZ
1216b Piper's Brook Road, Piper Brook,
Tasmania 7254. Tel: 3 6382 7066
Fax: 3 6382 7088. info@jansztas.com
www.jansz.com.au. Winemaker: various

PIPER'S BROOK VINEYARD
1216 Pipers Brook Road, Pipers Brook,
Tasmania 7254. Tel: 3 6382 7527
enquiries@pbv.com.au. www.pbv.com.au
Winemaker: Andrew Pirie

TALTARNI
60 Clover Hill Road, Lebrina, Tasmania
7254. Tel: 3 6395 6114. Fax: 3 6395 6257
info@taltarni.com.au. www.taltarni.com.au
Winemaker: Leigh Clarnette

VICTORIA
GIPPSLAND
BASS PHILLIP
Toschs Road, Leongatha South, Victoria
3953. Tel: 3 5664 3341. Fax: 3 5664 3209
Winemaker: Phillip Jones

YARRA VALLEY
COLDSTREAM HILLS
31 Maddens Lane, Coldstream, Vic 3770
Tel: 3 5964 9388
coldstream.hills@cellar-door.com.au
www.coldstreamhills.com.au
Winemakers: James Halliday, Philip Dowell

DE BORTOLI
Pinnacle Lane, Dixon's Creek, Vic 3775
Tel: 3 5965 2271. Fax: 3 5965 2442
yarra@debortoli.com.au
www.debortoli.com.au
Winemaker: Darren de Bortoli

DOMAINE CHANDON
Green Point, Maroondah Highway,
Coldstream, Vic 3770
Tel: 3 9739 1110. Fax: 3 9739 1095
postmaster@domainechandon.com.au
www.domainechandon.com.au
Winemakers: Dr Tony Jordan, Wayne
Donaldson

MOUNT MARY
Coldstream West Rd, Lilydale, Vic 3140
Tel: 3 9739 1761. Fax: 3 9739 0137
Winemaker: Dr John Middleton

TARRAWARRA VINEYARD
Healesville Rd, Yarra Glen, Vic 3775
Tel: 3 5962 3311. Fax: 3 5962 3887
enquiries@tarrawarra.com.au
www.tarrawarra.com.au
Winemaker: Clare Halloran

YARRA BURN
Settlement Road, Yarra Junction, Victoria
3797. Tel: 3 5967 1428. Fax: 3 5967 1146
cellardoor@yarraburn.com.au
www.yarraburn.com.au
Winemaker: Steve Flamsteed

YARRA YARRA
239 Hunts Lane, Steels Creek, Vic 3775
Tel: 3 5965 2380. Winemaker: Ian Maclean

YARRA YERING
Briarty Road, Coldstream, Victoria 3770
Tel: 3 5964 9267. Fax: 3 5964 9239
Winemaker: Bailey Carradus

YERING STATION
38 Melba Highway, Yering, Vic 3770
Tel: 3 9730 1107
info@yering.com
www.yering.com
Winemaker: Tom Carson

GEELONG
AUSTIN'S BARRABOOL
870 Steiglitz Rd, Sutherlands Creek, Vic
3331. Tel: 3 5281 1799. Fax: 3 5281 1673
abwines@abwines.com.au
www.abwines.com.au
Winemakers: John Ellis, Pamela Austin

BANNOCKBURN VINEYARDS
Midland Highway, Bannockburn, Vic 3331
Tel: 3 5281 1363
info@bannockburnvineyards.com
www.bannockburnvineyards.com
Winemaker: Gary Farr

BELLARINE
2270 Port Arlington Road, Bellarine, Vic
3222. Tel: 3 5259 3310. Fax: 3 5259 3393
www.bellarineestate.com.au
Winemaker: Robin Brockett

BY FARR
P.O. Box 72, Bannockburn, Vic 3331
Tel: 3 5281 1979. Winemaker: Gary Farr

JINDALEE
265 Ballan Road, Moorabool, North
Geelong, Vic 3221
Tel: 3 5276 1280. Fax: 3 5276 1537
www.jindaleewines.com.au
Winemaker: Andrew Byers

PROVENANCE WINES
870 Steiglitz Road, Sutherlands Creek, Vic
3331. Tel: 3 5272 2362
info@provenancewines.com.au
www.provenancewines.com.au
Winemaker: Scott Ireland

SCOTCHMANS HILL
190 Scotchmans Road, Drysdale,
Victoria 3222
Tel: 3 5251 3176. Fax: 3 5253 1743
info@scotchmans.com.au
www.scotchsmanshill.com.au
Chief winemaker: Robin Brockett

SHADOWFAX
K Road, Werribee, Victoria 3030. P.O.Box
209 Werribee
Tel: 3 9731 4420. Fax: 3 9731 4421
www.shadowfax.com.au
Winemaker: Matt Harrop

MORNINGTON PENINSULA
DROMANA ESTATE
13/143 Point Nepean Road, Dromana,
Victoria 3936. P.O.Box 417 Dromana
Tel: 3 5987 3177. Fax: 3 5987 3977
www.dromanaestate.com.au
Winemakers: Garry Crittenden, Rollo
Crittenden

RED HILL ESTATE
53 Redhill-Shoreham Rd, Red Hill South,
Vic 3937. Tel: 3 5989 2838
info@redhillestate.com.au
www.redhillestate.com.au
Winemaker: Micheal Kyberd

MAIN RIDGE ESTATE
80 William Rd, Red Hill, Vic 3937
Tel: 3 5989 2686. Fax: 3 5931 0000
mrestate@mre.com.au
www.mre.com.au
Winemaker: Nat White

STONIERS
362, Frankston-Flinders Road, Merricks,
Victoria 3916
Tel: 3 5989 8300. Fax: 3 5989 8709
stoniers@stoniers.com.au
www.stoniers.com.au
Winemaker: Geraldine McFaul

T'GALLANT
Mornington Road, Red Hill, Victoria 3937
Tel: 3 5989 6565. Fax: 3 5989 6577
info@tgallant.com.au
www.tgallant.com.au
Winemakers: Kathleen Quealy, Kevin
McCarthy

UPPER GOULBURN
DELATITE
Stoneys Road, Mansfield, Vic 3722
Tel: 3 5775 2922. Fax: 3 5775 2911
info@delatitewinery.com.au
www.delatitewinery.com.au
Winemakers: David and Rosalind Ritchie

TALLAROOK
2 Delaney's Road, Warranwood, Vic 3134
Tel: 3 9876 7022. Fax: 3 9876 7044
info@tallarook.com
www.tallarookwines.com.au
Winemaker: Scott McCarthy

BEECHWORTH
GIACONDA
McClay Rd, Beechworth, Vic 3747
Tel/Fax: 3 5727 0246
www.giaconda.com.au
Winemaker: Rick Kinzbrunner

PYRENEES & GRAMPIANS
BEST'S WINES
2 kms off Western Highway, Great
Western, Victoria 3377
Tel: 3 5356 2250. Fax: 3 5356 2430
www.bestswines.com
Winemakers: Viv Thomson, Hamish
Seabrook

BLUE PYRENEES
Vinoca Road (P.O.Box 3), Avoca,
Victoria 3647
Tel: 3 5465 3202. Fax: 3 5465 3259
www.bluepyrenees.com.au
Winemaker: Vicent Gere

DALWHINNIE
Taltarni Road, Moonambel, Victoria 3478
Tel: 3 5467 2388. Fax: 3 5467 2237
Winemaker: David Jones

MOUNT LANGI GHIRAN
Buangor-Ben Nevis Road, Buangor,
Victoria 3375
Tel: 3 5354 3207. Fax: 3 5354 3277
sales@langi.com.au
www.langi.com.au
Winemaker: Trevor Mast

TALTARNI
339 Taltarni Rd, Moonambel, Vic 3478
Tel: 3 5459 7900. Fax: 3 5467 2306
info@taltarni.com.au
www.taltarni.com.au
Winemaker: Peter Steer

GOULBOURN VALLEY & NAGAMBIE
MCPHERSON
PO Box 133, Goulburn Valley Highway,
Nagambie, Victoria 3608
Tel: 3 5794 2890. Fax: 3 5794 2805
www.mcphersonwines.com
Winemaker: Guido Vazzoler

MITCHELTON
Mitchellstown via Nagambie, Vic 3608
Tel: 3 5794 2710
mitchelton@mitchelton.com.au
www.mitchelton.com.au
Winemaker: Don Lewis

TAHBILK ESTATE
Tahbilk, Victoria, 3607
Tel: 3 5794 2555. Fax: 3 5794 2360
admin@tahbilk.com.au
www.tahbilk.com.au
Winemaker: Alister Purbrick

HEATHCOTE
HEATHCOTE WINERY
183-5 High Street, Heathcote, Vic 3523
Tel: 3 5433 2595. Fax: 3 5433 3081
winemaker@heathcotewinery.com.au
Winemaker: Mark Kelly

MACEDON RANGES
COBAW RIDGE
31 Perc Boyer's Lane, East Pastoria via
Kyneton, Vic 3444
Tel/Fax: 3 5423 5227
www.cobawridge.com.au
Winemaker: Alan Cooper

California

IRONY IN THE SITUATION, NOT IRON IN THE SOIL.

"If you want to keep on flying, you don't look down."
J.J.Cale.

PREVIOUS PAGE The Dry Creek bar/kitchen in Sonoma has a lot of old-fashioned charm but the food and wines are contemporary.

TOP High-powered juice transport arriving at the Mondavi Woodbridge winery; a sight to be seen in Lodi.

BELOW LEFT The two Louis Foppianos (father and son) drink their 1981 Petite Sirah under the winery walnut tree (photographed in October 2000).

BELOW RIGHT Old-style Californian wine bottles can be more seductive than anything contemporary.

Living and working amongst Easterners in 1969 it was striking, in so cosmopolitan and confident an island as Manhattan, that, the odd lunch companion apart, New Yorkers seemed united in regarding my affection for a daily dose of wine as weird. As weird indeed as I myself regarded, during that momentous year, in that aromatic, neck-stretching city, the natives' devotion to lunchtime highballs, tomato catsup, thin neckties, thin women, and tea bags. Enquiring of the local Greenwich Village liquor merchant, who liked wine, about his tiny selection of Californian bottles and what was worth buying, one was directed instead to the French section where the bargains and the big names were. Interstate taxes, he explained, made wines from California absurdly expensive; who would pay twelve bucks for something called Zinfandel when a single-vineyard burgundy could be had for eight?

In further visits to the Big Apple in the 1970s, little had changed except that a Stag's Leap Wine Cellar's Cabernet Sauvignon, from Napa, tasted on Long Island, struck this taster as exceptional. Also, around that time, interested Americans became aware that in 1976, at a widely reported comparative wine tasting held in Paris, a couple of Californians had thrashed the outraged French, who had, amongst other formidable bottles, fielded 1970 vintages of Châteaux Mouton-Rothschild and Haut Brion. One of those triumphant wines was a Cabernet Sauvignon from Stag's Leap. In 1981, during an extensive modern art research trip, a New York wine bar was discovered offering fancy Californians (expensively) by the glass. The most immediately arousing of these being from a bottle, the label impressing by its stark Soviet-poster-style typography, bearing the name Ridge.

It was an unforgettable wine, that Ridge. It was a Monte Bello Cabernet Sauvignon. It hit me as hard, as whimsically dramatically, as had my first encounter, in 1966, with so-called great wine, a 1947 Château Cheval Blanc. That Californians, people from a geologically perilous state who sprayed their oranges with toxins and worked on their movie-star tans on Christmas Day, could make such a wine was a revelation. This was now, without question, whatever I had tasted from there before, a place from which great wine could come and where imaginative winemakers existed. Yet how curious to find New Yorkers preferred their hard liquors to such things. But, as with everything, time has worked its magic and nowadays you can find NY wine merchants stocking over 500 Californian wines, with one offering everything from Cabernet Sauvignons such as Opus One 1998 at 400 bucks (£230) to Glen Ellen Reserve 2001 for $5.49 (£3.15).

This diversity is reflected in export markets overseas. In a hip UK restaurant, a Californian Merlot might be one of the house wines at £20 a bottle. In an even more up-market London eatery, a Harlan Cabernet Sauvignon from Oakville in the Napa will go for £250. Selfridges, the Oxford Street department store, will sell you a bottle of Screaming Eagle

TOP LEFT Monterey deputy sheriff, Dale E Smith, prepares to track the thieves who got away with valuable vineyard machinery.

TOP RIGHT There's almost nothing in California which doesn't carry an ad, announcement, or message. It's a proclamation culture, even down to the trucks delivering the grapes.

BELOW Why plant vines in California? Interrogate a local bunch of grapes. The answer is evident in every berry.

Cabernet Sauvignon, also from Oakville in the Napa, for something over £2,000. A Gallo red, on the other hand, will turn up on every UK supermarket shelf for around a fiver. In a few decades, the Californian wine industry has become a world-class player; a boutique business has turned itself into a major exporter, sufficiently combative and efficiently savvy enough to breathe down the necks of the French and Italians. True, much of this export success is helped by a weak dollar, for the first time allowing Californian wines to compete at the lower and middle levels with traditional European suppliers, but Californian wine is now on the map, writ large.

Drinkers, it seems, expect to pay a little more for a Cal bottle. Is it the sense of luxury it is perceived to exude? An extra sunniness of personality stemming from the outlooks of their makers? Even quite sober wine critics will refer to the "generosity" of Californian wines. It's as good a way as any to pigeon-hole them.

In California itself, however, they pigeon-hole themselves in a much more serious and gothically confusing way. The sheer taxonomic tediousness of it all is exhausting, with the so-called AVAs (Approved Agricultural Areas) so exasperatingly contrived – Carneros, for example, is an AVA in two counties, so it has its torso in Napa and two legs in Sonoma – that the wine drinker is not assisted in either making a precise judgement about provenance or quality. S/he is further confused by the looseness of label regulations which allow a grape variety to appear on the bottle yet contain up to twenty-five per cent of different varieties not even from the same county or sub-region. All you can really go on is the name of the producer; geography guarantees nothing you can smell or taste in the mouth. Central Valley, the biggest region of all, may not be highly regarded, but nearly three-quarters of all Californian wine grapes bask in its hot interior sun. It is Napa, however, accounting for around ten per cent of the acreage under vine, that basks in the cachet of the place a Californian wine grape would most like to be raised. On this tour of the vines, wines, and winemakers we will take in both places and also Sonoma, Carneros, Mendocino, Santa Cruz Mountains, Lodi, and Monterey.

Monterey
First the book. Then the movie.
Beginning here is, perhaps, an eccentric way to open, but blame my love for Steinbeck's *Cannery Row*. Monterey is its milieu and it is the novelist's greatest work, more complex, and less sentimental than *The Grapes of Wrath* for which he is famous. Modern Monterey, the sardine canneries long gone along with the sardine shoals, has evolved like abandoned docksides have all over the world, into a new spot for small businesses, restaurants, and shops to develop and prosper, tourists to flock, and local wineries to find new customers. Steinbeck, let alone Doc, the protagonist of the novel, would not recognize Ocean View Avenue,

which once boasted eighteen canning factories (one is now a trendy hotel), its name changed, in authorial homage, to Cannery Row (and, at number 400, the A Taste of Monterey wine shop and emporium). Local wineries have also benefited from the success of the 2005 Hollywood movie *Sideways*, about a winebuff and his sidekick discovering wayward sex and vinous thrills in the vineyards (even though these were mostly further south in Santa Barbara).

But grapes are not the biggest business here; lettuces are. In the local Salinas Valley (137 kilometres long, nineteen kilometres wide/eighty-five miles by twelve), where most of the grapes grow, green salads produce four crops a year and annual sales, just as raw produce, of over $1-billion (£0.57 billion).

In another historical sense, though, Monterey is the right place to start, however briefly, because it is where Paul Masson began (in 1852). This name was synonymous with Californian wine for decades. Now Monterey has other stalwarts such as Jekel, Calera, Estancia, Smith & Hook, J Lohr, Talbott, Lockwood, Chalone, and Ventana. Chardonnays, Viogniers, Chenin Blancs, Pinot Noirs, Cabernet Sauvignons, even Rieslings and Gewurztraminers from these have impressed over the years.

Lohr has its Cypress range of screwcapped wines. It also has a Painter Bridge Chardonnay and Zinfandel, the latter, at 13.5% ABV alcohol, is one of California's lighter expressions of this grape. It can show impressive raspberry/blackcurrant with good back-up tannins. Lohr's Crosspoint Pinot Noir, one of California's cheaper Pinots, has a teasing bouquet leading to fine expansive fruit. The best wines here are Riverstone Chardonnay, with its gobbets of orange-peel-tinged melon fruit and South Ridge Syrah (handsomely plummy).

A Talbott Chardonnay, from its Sleepy Hollow Vineyard in Gonzales, with its silky wood/fruit integration, once lubricated a memorable dinner in Carmel's Tutto Mondo restaurant. Mondavi has also picked some interesting grapes from its Bianchi vineyard holdings here and turned them into worthy wines.

On my first and only visit to this vineyard, there was deputy sheriff Dale E Smith kneeling in the dust looking at tyre tracks. A gang, likely as not from nearby Soledad, Gonzales, or Salinas – the angriest towns of the vast valley allotment – had broken into the vehicle store during the night and made off with prized machinery.

However, Sheriff Smith has investigated worse crimes. The nature of which reveal themselves as one drives through Salinas itself (where Steinbeck was born). The tidy dress of the local schoolchildren on the sidewalks is remarkable. There has been an official attempt to get all schoolkids into black pants and white shirts. Thirteen teenage murders in less than a year, all resulting from kids wearing gang colours to school, is the horrific inspiration. Hardly an encouraging environment in which to bring up youngsters, but a warm and sunny one (with, importantly, chilly nights courtesy of the nearby cold Pacific Ocean) in which to raise grapes.

Lodi

Large & Small

Flying through and over the immense early morning fog banks of Monterey to reach Lodi (in forty minutes), one can see why this area is, viticulturally, so valuable. The daytime sun is consistent, but it is that cold ocean – the cold air from which creates those banks – which keeps the clear nights chilly. The result is complex berries, as acids build up at night, sugars during the day.

There are less than a dozen producers in Lodi. The biggest, by far, is Mondavi Woodbridge. The smallest, and most compelling, is Lucas. They are connected with one another, for Paul Lucas, owner and winemaker of the 1,000-case winery, was also the viticultural boss of Mondavi. His is one of the most composed Zinfandels to have passed these lips.

Further south, in the San Joaquin Valley, lies the world's biggest single wine factory, Gallo at Modesto, with its own massive bottle-manufactory, and the somewhat smaller yet far more astonishing Andrew Quady of Quady Winery (who established himself some forty-four years after the Gallo Brothers in 1977). If you see the name Quady on a bottle (which will more than likely be a half-bottle) of rich dark liquid, you are in for a rare treat. These are Californian treasures, rich, deep, sweet, dessert-style, rhapsodic, fortified wines of massive unctuosity and honeyed depth. Quady's Essencia and Orange Muscat are simply wonderful and, if given five to ten years of bottle age, become amongst the world's most scrumptious sweet wines (and they are pretty amazing when young).

Santa Cruz Mountains
The Grahm & Draper show

With just under thirty producers, this is a small yet dynamic area which could merit a book by itself (along with several hundred rolls of my Fuji Provia-400 still camera film). Two significant problems, resistant of solution, are that as a named area it can get subsumed under the catch-all San Francisco Bay and the producers create wines from grapes which come from elsewhere. What is a Santa Cruz style? It all depends on the maker. I can only go on the makers and specific wines and these are Ahlgren Vineyard's Cabernet Sauvignon, Bargetto's Chardonnay, David Bruce's Zinfandel, Cinnabar's Cabernet Sauvignon, Cronin's Cabernet Sauvignon, Thomas Fogarty's Pinot Noir, Hallcrest's Riesling, Kathryn Kennedy's Merlot/Cabernet Franc, Mount Eden's Chardonnay, Page Mill's Chardonnay, Santa Cruz Mountain Vineyard's Pinot Noir, and Woodside's Gewurztraminer. And, towering above the lot (in depth of publicity if not always in depth of fruit) are the multifarious offerings bottled by Randall Grahm of the Bonny Doon Vineyard and the various blockbusters of Paul Draper at Ridge.

If there are two individuals who represent two distinct ways to portray the stirringly restless spirit of the passionate, creative Californian, it is demonstrated by the wines these two men create. There is rich irony in both men's souls and it far outweighs any mineral content, iron or anything else, which might be found in the soils of any vineyard from which they gather their grapes. One examines the wines, and they reveal all (for just as the fortune-teller needs only the palm and the astrologer the birth-chart, the vino-diviner needs only the wine in the glass). On this evidence, Grahm makes mistakes, is flirtacious, pugnacious, loves doing crosswords, and uses his Aquarian[1] instincts and senses to burn his way through a problem. Draper is intense, intellectual, hates meaningless trivia like shaving and chit-chat, is intuitive yet frighteningly well-focussed, and concentrates his intellectual energies on precise Piscean[2] targets. Their wines are more accurate depictions of each man's character as any portrait-in-oils or a report from a psychiatrist.

Grahm, after years of experimental failures with things like Pinot Noir, now concentrates on Rhône and Italian varieties. It is not always possible wholeheartedly to like all his wines, but the Roussanne and Marsanne blends and the Barbera have been challenging, witty, and immensely ambitious liquids which demonstrate the flair and dynamism of the man. Ca'del Solo Malvasia Bianca is intensely floral. Ca'del Solo Big House Red (screwcap) has cherries and plums and pert tannins and does indeed make a terrific house restaurant wine. Ancient Vines Carignan is wrinkle free in spite of the sun it flaunts. Le Cigare Volant, now the proud

---

[1] I know about as much about astrology as I do about changing car tyres.
[2] ditto

possessor of a screwcap, is meatily fruity and the tannins expand like a concertina in the mouth. Old Telegram, a blend of Mourvedre, Grenache, Carignan, and Syrah, is intense, civilized, smooth, textured like taffeta. His whackiest label in design terms is the screwcapped La Pousseur Syrah, a stunning hit of tobacco leaf and plummy ripeness with almost a hint of minestrone to its tannicity.

At Ridge, Paul Draper has also gone through a developmental cycle as the man has matured over the past thirty-five years or so of making the wines. Personally, I prefer the younger Draper's wines, even though the alcohol levels were pretty fierce, because they had a chutzpah unequalled by anything else in the State. His single vineyard bottlings of Zinfandel (Geyserville, Paso Robles, Lytton Springs), never wholly 100 per cent that grape, during the 1980s were bottles used in my household to astonish the sceptic, electrify the jaded, gobsmack the pedant who worshipped Bordeaux and/or the Rhône as a shrine and Barolo as a place of pilgrimage. Although for the claret hardnose the Ridge Monte Bello Cabernet Sauvignon, being of the Bordeaux grape, was a sharper weapon, when five or six years old, with which instantaneously to cut out the canker of deep seated prejudice. The Ridge Santa Cruz Mountains Chardonnay is also a superb wine, proud, assertive, not afraid to shout Wood! But with the fruit to answer back. A Santa Cruz Mountains Cabernet/Merlot/Petit Verdot is also a confident wine of great style. Of the Zinfandels of the 2000-decade, my favourite is the 2001 Lytton Springs Sonoma, which is seventy-four per cent Zin, eighteen per cent Carignan, and eight per cent Petite Sirah with almost a cherry liqueur edge to its tannins. On some of the other Zins, the high alcohol peeped through the fruit and was not an elegant sight.

Santa Barbara
A fine trio
At Au Bon Climat, the owner, Jim Clendenen, has used the knowledge he gained in the 1980s working in Burgundy with Chardonnay and Pinot Noir to create one of the State's most consistent wineries for these varieties. Wild Boy Chardonnay has the caressing texture a Meursault grower would die for. Santa Barbara County Chardonnay has more character and bite. Talley Chardonnay made from fruit from Arroyo Grande in San Luis Obispo, is simply gorgeous, unguent, a balm for the tongue. Sanford & Benedict Pinot Noir is accomplished, with a slow gamey richness, well textured. La Bauge Pinot Noir has even finer gamey raspberries and tannins. But the beast, the elixir, one of the sassiest Pinots in the State, is Rosemary Pinot Noir (also made from Talley vineyard fruit). 2001, for example, was one of the finest Californian Pinots I tasted in 2005 with a crunchily gorgeous gaminess and rich tannins making it wonderfully slow moving and lightly molten.

At Qupé, the Bien Nacido range is the most vigorous, with a Viognier/Chardonnay, a Reserve Syrah, and a Hillside Select Syrah. These are challenging wines of class and concentration, demonstrating maker Bob Lindquist to be a man of principle and ambition. He also produces what must surely be the only Albariño (the Spanish white grape of Galicia) made in the state. The wines have superb textures. Always the mark of a winemaker who understands Life with a large L.

The Fess Parker Winery was famous before it starred, under the name Frass Winery, in the Hollywood film *Sideways*. Fess Parker was a famous actor of the black and white TV days, his role being to portray backwoods hero Davy Crockett, and so the winery can resemble a geriatric retreat during the tourist season as folks with long memories and square eyes come to pay their respects to old Davy. The wines are made by son Eli and his Santa Barbara Pinot Noir is potent stuff, sometimes getting towards 15% ABV, and it'll put new lead in any geriatric's pencil with its craggy texture and virile tannins.

Napa Valley
Statuesque

Years ago, on a fleeting visit to the Mondavi winery in Napa, Michael Mondavi insisted I tasted a Château Latour alongside his top-level reds to demonstrate the superiority of the Mondavi Reserve range. He was urged not to open the absurdly pricey Latour, but to no avail. In any case, this taster needed no convincing of Mondavi's finesse and breeding in this regard. Father, Bob Mondavi (born 1913), has done as much as anyone, and more than most, to make Californian wine a world contender and the family's Reserve wines are not only good, but at times outstanding.

For though Gallo was the biggest Californian producer, and the most dynamic on world export markets, Mondavi made expressive, characterful wines, many at accessible prices. Gallo manufactured jug wines and didn't even put a vintage date on a bottle until the late 1970s. Bob Mondavi, on the other hand, was running around Burgundy in the 1960s and, as a result, this fed through to new barrel regimes and vineyard management ideas back home in Napa. The man was an unselfish visionary.

But by the new millennium, though still a virile, opinionated individual (his sons helped run the show day to day), Robert Mondavi was a personality to be wheeled out (or more graphically, an elderly Lion to be uncaged) at important functions. Bob was the star of the show, and Tim Mondavi was the number one disciple; both were fawned over by PR people and junior staff like father-and-son religious gurus by adoring acolytes. As Tim, in charge of winemaking (brother Michael was chairman, Bob chairman emeritus), spoke through his froth of cappuccino-coloured beard – resembling in tone and liquidity a beverage become fluent – his father told stories like a clean-shaven Moses.

For weren't the Mondavis like aristocrats in Napa? They had already diversified into so-called super-wine with the setting up of the Opus One winery in Napa with joint-proprietor Baron Rothschild of Bordeaux. This

TOP LEFT Heather Patterson, viticulturalist at Keyes Vineyard, Howell Mountain, is a mite concerned.

TOP RIGHT Fingertip precision at Hartford Court winery, Sonoma.

BELOW LEFT Tim Mondavi expresses himself with fluent hands.

BELOW RIGHT When Jesse Jackson, lawyer, bought his first vineyard in 1981, did he know it would one day grow into the mighty Kendall-Jackson company, now farming over 4,860 hectares of wine grapes in California?

was as much an ego-exercise for the Mondavis, as it was a whole-hearted business decision. They wanted to be seen as a premier league wine family (and even joined an international chapter of such familial groupings). Opus One has never been the wine its makers tried to make it or trumpet it as being. It was always expensive, but rarely better, to this palate, than some examples of the much cheaper Mondavi Reserve range. Mondavi also went into joint-projects overseas, notably in Chile. Other brands owned or co-owned were Ornellaia, Luce della Vite, Lucente, Arrowood, La Famiglia di Robert Mondavi, Hang Time, Byron, and Caliterra. In 2000, it splashed $28 million (£16 million) on a new winery with open-topped wooden fermenters, massively expensive equipment, because it wanted to ape burgundy.

This was an impressive commitment, but one weighted towards the premium end of the market. The balance of such a portfolio is easily endangered if cash flow is sluggish. Standing tall and keeping your head held high is impressive, but not if you neglect to keep your feet on the ground. In going public (in 1993) the Mondavi empire, though a

significant shareholding lay in family hands, was beholden to shareholders. Yet as a family entity with a public share price it lasted barely as long as the Third Reich. In September 2004, the company, squeezed financially, announced it was to divest itself of its luxury assets and concentrate on its core portfolio of cheaper wines. It laid off a third of its Napa workforce, 360 employees in all (doubtless some of those fawning PR people amongst them). Equally hard to swallow (just like an Opus One at two hundred bucks the bottle), was the company's decision to sell its Napa vineyards and divest itself of its interests in overseas wineries.

The world's biggest wine conglomerate, Constellation Brands, saw its chance. It could surely make an offer the shareholders would find irresistible in preference to a lengthy and not necessarily hugely profitable bit-by-bit sell-off. It could swallow Mondavi whole. The deal cost Constellation more than a billion dollars (£0.57 billion) and it ensured all Robert Mondavi brands – from the $5 (£2.87) Woodbridge wines made at Lodi to the $125 (£72) Robert Mondavi Napa Cabernet Sauvignon Reserve – were not sold separately. The Mondavi board of directors, including family members, voted unanimously to sell. In one fell swoop, Constellation had become world number one, able to boast of producing eighty million cases of wine annually (as against Gallo's seventy million).

Wine is in the blood

So a dynasty falls (or is absorbed and loses its individuality). But the Mondavi name, as a brand, will be retained (to expunge it would be an act of insanity as irrational as brand owners BMW phasing out the Rolls Royce or Mini names). Robert Mondavi himself, with his nonagenarian brother Peter and son Tim, will still make wine as the family has announced a joint venture together. The Mondavis have an unquenchable thirst to put their personalities into wine bottles.

What will one miss, though, with the end of the Mondavi empire? There is huge entertainment value in ambition and the Mondavis had ambition in bucket loads; it showed wholly in the wines. Only an American, perhaps only a Californian, could worship ritual and romance so passionately, so religiously. That's what made a good few of the wines so challenging: they were completely and unashamedly pretentious.

This was never more perfectly exemplified than at the Opus One winery, where from the classical references in the architecture to the *faux* Louis XIV reception room, the attempt was made to give the impression of antiquity and true class, just as the Victorian railway termini builder created the superficial impression of a temple in order to reassure travellers the transport system was solid and safe. If you asked an awkward question of the curator at Opus One, you were made to feel a bit like a visitor who steps out of line in the Vatican to hassle the Pope.

Napa itself is like a shrine. The name helps: those two decisive, haughty syllables. And it is beautiful, in parts: the light, the vines in autumn, the hills, and some of the wines are breathtakingly civilized. One must learn to ignore things like the silly statuary at the Mondavi Oakville headquarter vineyards, echoed in some other wineries by extravagant add-ons, as just Californian kitsch, and as no more indicative of the food in the dish as the linoleum on the table-top, and try to concentrate on those wines. But it is hard. And it is hard because some of the wines incorporate those symbols of wealth and showiness; they have absorbed such parvenu insecurities into their fabrics. Faced as they are in the wider world by the intimidating presences of the Old World's French, Italian, Spanish, German, and Portuguese producers' perceived mastery of certain wine styles, no matter how thumpingly a Napa wine might beat one or all of them hollow in a blind tasting, it is not enough. You can hang a medal around anyone's neck, or the neck of a bottle, but you can't alter the neck's origin. It will need another couple of generations of drinkers to have passed well into their dotages, and American reverence for certain things European to be supplanted by other concerns (Chinese culture perhaps, almost certainly Russian golfers and Indian movie stars), before California as a whole, even Napa as a specific vineyard area of obvious world-class status, feels wholly comfortable in its skin.

The Power of metaphors

Napa wines, even as the third millennium is well under way, still aspire to a comparative exemplary excellence seen to exist elsewhere. We are all implicated in the conspiracy every time we say of a local Cabernet, as recourse to a handy metaphor, that it's like a jammy Pauillac. When the day comes that Latour sees fit to pit its wine against a Napa Cabernet saying "we think we've really cracked it this time", is the day the New World revolution will have truly been won.

Until then, we, can delight in Napa wines from the slickest producers, aware that though these guys have addresses in Napa, this is not true of each and every wine that they make. One of the biggest differences between European and New World producers is that the former's business address, where they press the grapes, is almost invariably the region where they also gather the grapes; with New World producers, with their greater freedom, they can pick grapes outside their region, Sonoma say or in Mondavi's case some wines bear its name as far away as Lodi or Monterey (though of course they will not mask origin by misleading labelling). Napa itself seems to have at least eleven vaguely geographical sub-areas within its fifty-six kilometre length and six kilometre width (thirty-five miles by four wide): Howell Mountain; Calistoga; Chiles Valley; Spring Mountain; Saint Helena; Rutherford; Oakville; Atlas Peak; Stag's Leap; Yountville; and Mount Veeder – oh yes, and a chunk of Carneros too don't forget. But how? A line-up of wines, Cabernets or Chardonnays say, from all eleven or twelve areas, would not necessarily demonstrate a dozen styles of wine from the same grape. How the wine is made, remember, is far more telling than where the grapes were grown, though without doubt a local expert might be able to make one or two educated guesses. It would be surprising if it were otherwise. There are over 200 producers in the Valley and they run from the daring to the delicate, the vulgar to the vivacious.

Some of the best

Araujo in Calistoga makes truly compelling Cabernet and Shiraz. Cakebread in Rutherford surprises with a Sauvignon Blanc that, with a little bottle age, exhibits a challenging complexity (it produces Cabernets and Merlot also). Caymus makes a barrel-aged Cabernet which is lush but not OTT in cooler vintages. Chateau Montelena turns out a crisp Chardonnay which seems more northern Italian than Napa, but its Cabernet Sauvignon can be very finely tuned indeed. Clos du Val has made a toothsome Cabernet at times. Clos Pegase boasts an impressive winery, but less ornate liquids. Cuvaison has shown itself capable of turning out a beautifully plummy Merlot. Dalla Valle's Cabernets used to have tannins you could eat with a fork, but these have calmed down in the recent past. Darioush has a smart winery but I've not tried the wines. Diamond Creek in Calistoga lives up to its name, pricewise, but aims to make long-living Cabernets – indeed it makes the claim that it is Napa's first exclusively Cabernet estate – from three sites and the vines are beautiful to behold with their hillside curvature and symmetry. (How can you make a good living selling just 3,000 cases of wine a year? Easy. Charge 150 bucks a bottle). Dominus, owned by Bordeaux négociant Christian Mouiex in Yountville, turns out neatly tailored Inglenook Cabernets. Duckhorn's eponym, Dan, makes, amongst other things, a richly engaging Pinot Noir from fruit sourced from the Anderson Valley and, engaging us further with Bonny-Doon-like punning, a Napa Valley red, seventy-five per cent Zinfandel, called Paraduxx. This last can exhibit some delightfully challenging tannins. At Franciscan, owned by Constellation, there is an often highly flavoured so-called Cuvée Sauvage

Chardonnay, made with natural yeasts. The penchant for puns can also be found at Frog's Leap, in Rutherford, with a wine, I confess I have yet to taste, called Leapfrogmilch. If it is anything like owner John Williams's other wines it will be confident and surprisingly stylish. His mainstream wines, made organically and with naturally-occurring yeasts, are superb: Carneros Chardonnay is stunningly complete and elegant; Napa Valley Zinfandel is played *legato* with a lovely prickle of *sostenuto* tannins; the Napa Valley Cabernet is even more musically fine, sustained, subtle, highly melodic and integrated; and his Rutherford Cabernet Sauvignon, with five or six years of bottle age, is remarkably polished yet characterful.

The Croatian Californian

Such epithets also characterize the wines made by Mike Grgich at Grgich Hill Cellars in Rutherford. Indeed, it was he who made one of the wines, a 1973 Napa Chardonnay, that beat the French in the 1976 blind tasting referred to in my introduction to this California section. Meeting the man is an enlightening, oft time challenging experience as he tells the story of his long walk to freedom from Croatia to arrive in California in the 1950s (he crossed the ocean under someone else's steam one presumes) and his Chardonnay can, at times, be the most restrained, most subtle, most gloriously delicate yet emphatic in the state. This is wholly to do with his methods which, for one thing, permit no malolactic fermentation to occur in the wine. This results in a leaner style, as the appley malic acids in the wine have not been transformed into the milky lactic acids that are the norm, to a greater or lesser extent, with other Chardonnays. The finesse of his Chardonnays is sometimes breathtaking.

At Harlan Estate in Oakville, it is the prices of the organic Cabernets that take one's breath away. The cheapest London restaurant price, at Andrew Edmunds in Soho, is a mere £150 a bottle for the 1996 vintage. The 1994, however, was said to be one of the most complete Napa Cabernets ever made, but alas, I have not tasted it (please note Mr Harlan: the publisher has my delivery address). Somewhere in the States a collector has a dozen bottles, bought from Christie's Auction House in Rockerfeller Plaza New York in April 2005 for £352 each.

Pointing up the bewildering nature of the geography and vineyard location in Napa is the famous Saintsbury winery, named after a famous literary wine bore. It is in Napa, indubitably, but it's also in Los Carneros Avenue, Carneros, which because the AVA's are agricultural areas rather than administrative ones (like the counties are within the state) means you always have to think twice. But there it is, a proud Napa Pinot beacon, matchless in its committment to that grape (Saintsbury also grows Chardonnay). David Graves and Richard Ward, after twenty odd years of turning out consistently finely wrought Pinots, show no signs of flagging in their enthusiasm. Their Carneros Reserve Chardonnay can, in some vintages, play second fiddle to no other.

CALIFORNIA

Two Stags. One leap

Further confusion exists in Napa with the winery with two names, or is it two with the same name (almost)? It is the latter. Stags' Leap Winery is at 6150 Silverado Trail and Stag's Leap Wine Cellars is at 5766. There is "only a wire fence between the properties", one is informed (and the evidence is there to see), but to the wine snob it is the latter which has more prestige because it is owned by Warren Winiarski and not the Fosters subsidiary Beringer-Blass like the other one. Yet both turn out excellent wines.

Stags' Leap Winery makes a terrific Cabernet Sauvignon, which in 2001 at least, was better than its rival's. It also has a terrific Rhône blend – to out-Aussie the Aussies – called Ne Cede Malis and, its benchmark red, a Petite Sirah of great vivacity and presence, showing bacon-edged richness allied to assertive tannins. Stag's Leap Wine Cellars (note the apostrophe, it's crucial) has its Hawk Crest range, but more provocative are the Napa Valley Artemis Cabernet Sauvignon, beautifully structured, elegantly attired in silky tannins, and Fay Vineyard Cabernet Sauvignon, which is smooth, contented, almost a trifle smug.

At Mayacamas, there is made a nicely wrought, unneurotic Chardonnay and Cabernet Sauvignon which can be most unNapa-like. It is said this is because the vineyards are at such a high elevation, but it is more likely to be the resolute character of Bob Travers, who owns the estate. He is no Napa groupie. Neither is Peter Newton. His Newton Estate, as befits someone born in Britain with its tradition of amazing gardeners, has superbly well-tailored vineyards, though this owes a lot to the layout skills of his wife, Su Hua. The Chardonnay and Cabernet Sauvignon from here show a neatness, a cohesion, a harmony every bit reflected in the estate itself and the owners' finesse.

At Niebaum-Coppola there is pizzazz rather than finesse. The so-called Diamond range is ripe and clotted but the flagship Rubicon is not easily crossed with its exuberant jamminess. Subtle these wines are not.

Plumpjack has more cheek, for it was the first premium Napa producer to offer a Reserve Cabernet in a choice of screwcap or cork. It isn't just a winery – though with its picturesque twenty hectares of vines given a degree of charm by the views of the surrounding Mayacamas and Vaca Mountains, it is a beautiful one – it is a big business (to be expected, as the major shareholder is the Getty family). It not only makes dramatic gestures with its wines, like Tessa's Cuvée Chardonnay in honour of Tessa Newsom, who died of breast cancer in 2002, profits going to a cancer support group, it also has restaurants in the state, sports shops, and the winery itself even boasts a Beer Club.

Mount Veeder is more discrete though its owner is even richer than the Gettys. Constellation is the world's largest wine company, and it lets Mount Veeder get on with producing some excellent wines. The Cabernet Sauvignon shows remarkably fine tannins.

Even more discrete than this is Kent Rasmussen. When I first met him he offered me, from his garage, a glass of Pinotage. It was, he said, from the last vines in the state as phylloxera, the vine-louse, had got to them and they had to be grubbed up. On behalf of the whole Cape wine industry I breathed a sigh of relief. The Pinotage was sublime. As are his wonderful Pinot Noirs from Carneros. He makes wines from several grapes, including Italian varieties, and bottles them under the Ramsay label, but his own-name labelled Pinots can be amongst the most delicately perfumed, most gamily serene in the State.

Screaming Eagle (*see* California introduction), named after a Harley-Davidson motorbike, is a boutique establishment with just a few hectares of Cabernet vines and an annual production of around 500 cases. Its luxury market is, I would imagine, twenty-three year-old Silicon Valley software trillionaires who have been brought up on cola and need a ravishingly expensive juice with which to celebrate Sundays round the pool.

At Sutter Home, it's party time every day as the hugely entertaining Trinchero family celebrate their rise to enormous wealth on the back of creating white Zinfandel. They now have the fourth largest winery in California creating this disgusting confection, which is in fact pink, though that kind of derogatory remark only makes them chuckle. I had a lovely family dinner at the Trinchero homestead some years back and ate a duck one of the family had shot while out hunting. With it went a Trinchero Family Reserve Cabernet which was utterly and completely mesmerizingly deliciously perfect with the dish.

Turley Wine Cellars is celebrated for creating Zinfandel and Petite Sirah blends of ferocious jamminess. Only once have I tasted a wine from this estate. It was an experience to swallow, so clotted, so ripe, so puppy-dog-eager was it. They do not make wines here, one must say, for the refined palate. Until I experienced a Turley wine I did not know I could lay claim to one (having always regarded my palate as rustic).

The power of a name

What one must recognize above all is that Napa carries a cachet which has nothing to do with the way the wine performs on the palate (or the insecurity of those living there). Californians, interested Americans (not to mention wine collectors world-wide), see Napa as certain soccer supporters see the turf at Manchester United's Old Trafford or dandies a particular tailor in Savile Row. As a shrine. As something almost holy. There is no rationality involved in such reverence. It is possible to set a Napa wine down next to wines from Moldova, Romania, China, Morocco, even Egypt (well, maybe Egypt's stretching the point a bit) and each might be more congenial than the one from Napa. But only one wine comes from Napa and can say so. That's what counts. That's what, for many people who drink labels with their eyes rather than judge wines with their tastebuds, is worth the money. Any car can take you from A to B. But hasn't the woman in the Ferarri got the edge? Somehow?

However with some Napa wines one is reminded of the historian Duff Cooper's judgement on the nineteenth century post-revolutionary French leader Barras who "possessed bravado without courage, cunning rather than cleverness, joviality rather than humanity, and swagger rather than elegance". Without the Napa Valley, not only would the American wine industry be immeasureably poorer, but the world of wine would lack a great treasure.

Do Californian women make different wine from Californian men?
If the theme of this book holds water, then it follows that women would make different wine from men (even from the same grapes from the same vineyard). As far as I know, and I have searched, there is no vineyard in the world which is shared between winemakers of different sexes and so we cannot compare their wines and come to a judgement. However, in California there are winemakers whose wines not only echo their makers' personalities, but because those personalities are women, bequeath

qualities to the wines which only a woman could pass on. One obvious way in which this is demonstrated is in aroma, in a wine's bouquet. Many a man makes a wine indifferently scented, but no woman does. Can you imagine a woman making a wine which did not have a distinctive, however discrete, perfume of its own?

When the beautifully fluent Heather Pyle made wine for the Mondavis at La Famiglia winery (she left some years ago), why was it that her liquids were so different from the Mondavi norm? Was it just the Italian varieties the winery specialized in? Or her deft touch with soft words which resulted in such soft wines? Heather characterized her gorgeous Sangiovese, for example, as a "chameleon wine, changing as it develops and matures". She went on to describe how she felt it was a wine that metamorphosed to suit the background of food with which it was paired, and having tasted it with various dishes, I entirely concur with her imagery. No man would ever think about his wine in this pragmatic way.

When father Robert and son Tim Mondavi speak about wine, for example, we encounter incorrigible romantics not given to congenial animal analogies. They are possessed of the idea that there is wine and there is great wine and the creation of the latter is an artistic process. I refute the separation of wine into categories, there is only wine, and I firmly mistrust the idea of the liquid itself having any connection with art. Such a fallacious line of argument elevates the practitioners of the skill of wine-growing and the craft of winemaking into artists. This is a meretricious idea and swallowing it bad for the brain; for if wine is artistic then we are forced to accept its flaws as artistic expressions and not mistakes for which we should be refunded the price of the bottle.

Gina Gallo is also eloquent on the subject of her job, which is making wine, and her very name evokes the notion of male grandiosity because her late grandfather Julio and his still active brother Ernest are legends. They created the world's second largest wine company, E & J Gallo of Modesto California, where Gina grew up. Until recently, the Gallo winery in Modesto turned out more wine in a year than was produced annually in the whole of Australia. I do not find this fact, or the wines from this vast plant, remotely as interesting as grand-daughter Gina's wickedly seductive bottles. Why? Because her heart is in her wines, whereas there is only an anonymous accountant's in the wines from the Modesto manufactory.

Her wines come from vineyards further north than Modesto in Sonoma county. They have given the Gallo name a partial status but not everyone is keen to acknowledge it. Conspiring in huddled groups at tastings, certain British wine critics turn up their noses at bottles with the Gallo name on them. I have seen these wretched snobs, unable to bring any independent judgement to bear, ignore a sublimely delicious Cabernet Sauvignon on these grounds. I once overheard a well known wine correspondent remark to another that, "I couldn't possibly taste this wine, could you, Daedalus?

TOP LEFT In the days when Heather Pyle made La Famiglia wines for the Mondavi family, the liquids were as poised, approachable, and as complex as she was.

TOP RIGHT From some of Sonoma's most carefully tended vines, Gina Gallo turns out the most ambitious reds to bear the Gallo name.

BELOW LEFT Gina Gallo swallows some of her own robust medicine.

BELOW RIGHT Tim Mondavi and father Robert, towering figures in the Californian wine industry, contemplate a future as no longer managing eponyms of the Mondavi empire (now owned by Constellation, the world's largest wine conglomerate).

It's a Gallo bottle." Daedalus, gentleman that he is, took the easy way out and agreed with her. The wine was one of Gina's. It was Gallo Sonoma Barelli Creek Cabernet Sauvignon 1996.

On visits to California I have tasted this wine several times, drunk it with food, and found it a most impressively complete Cabernet Sauvignon. And I tasted on those trips, let me tell you, some of California's fanciest and most preposterously male hormonal Cabernet Sauvignons – by which I mean that the buyer has to dig very deep into his pocket to acquire them.

California is much the same size as Bordeaux with around 120,000 hectares of vines. Unfortunately some of the wine-growers, particularly in Napa, grow more than grapes; they foster the idea that blights Bordeaux – that wine is not so much a joy but a religion.

What is Gina Gallo's view of the male idea that making wine is artistry? "Well, wine can't be an artistic expression, because such a thing would be unique, a one-off, whereas wine clearly isn't," she once calmly pointed out to me (in a bar in Healdsville).

Another famous wine woman in Sonoma county also carries (possibly) the burden of a name. Marimar Torres is sister of the man who runs Spain's largest independent wine company, Miguel Torres. She was once married to a wine critic (the dullest adventure upon which a woman can embark, I would have thought). She has studied viticulture and she has a business degree from Stanford University and speaks not only her native Catalan and Spanish, but also German, French, and Italian. And English.

She is also an avid collector of cutlery. I had never met one before. She finds most of her knives and forks and spoons six miles high. For Marimar's cutlery (or "silverware" as it states unequivocally on the drawer which holds the knives and forks in her kitchen where everything is labelled) is exclusively the donation of various airlines on which she has flown first or business class.

LEFT DeLoach of Santa Rosa makes terrific wines from the Russian River Valley and, if you're passing, the winery is an education to visit.

CENTRE LEFT Mistress of all she surveys: Marimar Torres's Chardonnays and Pinots Noirs express themselves with passion and polish (as she does in half-a-dozen languages).

CENTRE RIGHT The Russian River Valley is a perfectly sited niche in which to grow wine grapes.

RIGHT A warning to passing motorists from the organically-minded citizens of Hopland, Mendocino: trees are more valuable than automobiles and they never become obsolete.

Thus, dinner with her was accomplished, on my part, with a Finnair knife and fork for the main course, while the dessert utensils came courtesy of Delta. My breakfast fork, next day, was marked British Airways; the dinner things that night announced JAL (discretely – you have to search for these names).

Why would a woman who has access to enough money to last several lifetimes, who owns several homes, assiduously collect airline silverware? I asked her. She shrugged; looked puzzled, as though the answer was obvious. "Well," she finally said, "I just thought it would be fun to kit out the kitchen of the winery house like this. I'd ask every airline I flew on for a souvenir and they always obliged and now, as you can see, I have a whole silverware drawer full."

Control – a place for everything and everything in its place – is Marimar's passion. Everything has a sign on it, often in two languages. The vines obligingly tell you which grapes they are growing and what clone they are. The offices, the houses, even the bedroom of the guest house where I slept, had signs everywhere telling me not to do this, to put this there, to remember to strip the bed when I leave and put the sheets in the utility room. This is the moral universe of a dynamic, hugely-talented, self-confessed control freak. I wondered, though I did not ask, if she ever went in to the vineyard and "had a word" with the vines. I have no doubt that were she to do so the vines would sit up and listen and instantly obey.

"Teamwork produces the wine and the grapes are partners in that," she says. Could any man so generously concede the human element which dominates terroir?

In the millennial year I drank only five truly great and gripping wines from the Pinot Noir grape: Bass Phillip South Gippsland 1995 (from Australia), Domaine Leroy Pommard 1994 (Burgundy), René Engel Echézeaux 1989 (Burgundy), Zind-Humbrecht Pinot d'Alsace 1990, and Marimar's 1992. The perfume of the latter was to die for.

How to make a colossal fortune in the wine industry?
Start out with a tiny one
Lunch with Mr and Mrs Jackson in London (Le Gavroche) was an inspiring few hours. "Jess, you know," said Mrs Jackson, "will disappear shopping for a few hours and, unlike most men who might come back with a new tie or even a set of golf clubs, he returns with a winery in his pocket." Livens up a marriage I suppose.

To begin with, lawyer Jess Jackson's first vineyard acquisition in 1982, Lake County, was a modest affair. But then the buying spree took place, and so shrewdly that Jackson Family Vineyards became Kendall-Jackson, owning by the late 1990s Edmeades, Hartford Court, Lokoya, Pepi, La Crema, Stonestreet, Cambria, and Matanzas Creek. It farms over 4,800 hectares of vines. La Crema Pinot Noir is Kendall-Jackson's most strikingly feral red wine. The winery in Geyserville went bust in 1993 and Jess snapped it up. La Crema also makes a Sonoma Coast Chardonnay which is quite lovely in its plumpness yet lithe finish, but it's the three Pinot Noirs, from the Sonoma Coast, Carneros, and Russian River Valley, which take centre stage – as with any vintage one or other comes out on top with that wild raspberry gaminess so alluring in the grape. Lately, it's been the Carneros. Years back, it was the Russian River.

I have no doubt that Jess Jackson would have become the largest proprietor of Californian wines and vineyards had not Constellation come along. What will happen, though, when Jess gets bored with all these toys? It is impossible to predict.

Sonoma
Poorer cousin
Sonoma Valley is only a little way north of Napa, yet its grapes average $1,000 (£573) less a ton. That helps explain why Napa-grown wines are never cheap and why, if you're a Napa producer and want to introduce a cheaper range, you source the fruit elsewhere. In the New World, grapes travel – and mostly they travel well.

The Ravenswood winery shows another aspect of modern winemaking: the so-called "hands off" approach. The winemaker, Joel Peterson, has a relationship with Zinfandel to which the obsession of Galahad with Guinevere was mere dalliance. As a result, he proceeds delicately and employs a light hand, uses local yeasts and does not filter the wines. The owner, the massive Constellation corp, also keeps a low profile, seeming to let the winemaker get on with producing a range of successful Zinfandels from the accessible Vintners Blend range to complex potencies like the Ravenswood Lodi Old Vine Zinfandel with its delicious bitter cherry and liquorice fruit.

Simi is another Sonoma winery owned by Constellation, but the wines here have changed since winemaker Zelma Long left (and went to ply her trade in South Africa). The Cabernet from the Alexander Valley lacks the oomph of a Ms Long wine, but is very smooth and ripely attractive.

At the Peter Michael Winery they like high prices and adore high alcohols. The main man here, Peter Michael, made his money in the UK in electronics and moved to California, his vines producing their first wine crop in 1987. The wines are overwhelming. The Mon Plaisir Chardonnay, 15% ABV, shows very evident upbeat French wood and L'Esprit de Pavots, a Cabernets Franc and Sauvignon and Merlot blend, with its towering 15.5% ABV was, in the 2001 vintage at least, a wine to sip judiciously. The La Carriere Chardonnay 2002, however, was a nigh perfect example of the wood wrought style and I rated it 19 points out of 20 at its UK retail price of £52.27. This is a hugely ambitious estate. And a confusingly located one. Is it in Napa, but the address is in Calistoga. Is it in Sonoma? Depending on which local expert you ask you can be told either.

Arrowood, in Glen Ellen, makes not just interesting Chardonnays and Viogniers, but also late-harvest wines from Riesling. I was sitting next to Richard Arrowood in 2000 in Napa when he broke the news that he had sold out to Mondavi (thence to Constellation); and this impressive wine-talker looked like the cat who'd not just got the cream, but the mouse with it. Is he smiling now? No reason why not. Constellation's involvement and backing will not, if other wineries are anything to go by, mean stupid interference, but letting the winemakers get on with the job of expressing themselves. Before Arrowood, Richard was the winemaker at Sonoma's Chateau St Jean and he created wines there, from Sauvignon and Chardonnay, of dazzling texture and concentration.

Clos du Bois in Geyserville, with its late 1980s Chardonnays, was among this taster's favourite Californian white wines. A couple of times the wines had a few years of bottle age under their belts and were certainly all the better for it. This was also true of the Zinfandels tasted from the DeLoach winery. Cecil DeLoach made a speciality of Zinfandel and his oak-aged wines can be tremendous. At Duxoup, another Californian punster exists in the shape of Andrew Cutter. His Syrah is jammy and lively.

For more old-style Zin, with Petite Sirah, the place to head for is Foppiano in Healdsburg. The craggy style is in force here, robust and full-on, and with a hearty casserole these sunny wines can be a treat – the wines put the boot in, they do not go on tip-toe. The opposite is true of Don Hartford's wines at Hartford Court in Forestville (owned by Kendall-Jackson). I recall staying overnight at the winery whilst Don, whose wife Jennifer is Jess Jackon's daughter, went out to a wine show dinner to pick up a major award. The wines were there to console me, however, and a most enjoyably complex Zinfandel and a delicate Pinot Noir compensated for mine host's absence.

At Kistler, in Sebastopol, the care put into the winemaking shows too. There were some wonderful late 1990s Chardonnays made here which really showed that rare quality of being pulled from the earth. It does take meticulous, subtle winemaking techniques to create that impression and Steve Kistler has it.

Healdsburg

Job anyone?

Here I am in the pretty town of Healdsburg, where the property prices are going through the roof and where the more successful local wine makers like to live. It's 8.30 on a foggy October morning and on the corner of Center Street where it runs by the northern end of the town's central plaza, small groups of Mexican casual workers are still waiting for work, hoping (against hope on this particular day as it turns out) that a vineyard manager will cruise by in his pick-up truck and say "hop in boys, today we're pickin' grapes." Or rather, as is more likely, "Muchachos, ustedes trabajo hoy!"

I wander the town, pay a few visits, strike up several conversations with its civilized citizens, have a lone lunch in a cosy joint which shares its toilet facilities with the town's cinema. No wonder winemakers like to live here. Come the afternoon the wanabee workers are still there, still kicking their heels. The sun is now up, it's 25°C (77°F), the fog has lifted. The wanabees have moved from the street corners. They're sitting on the benches under the plaza's majestic redwoods. There's an older Mexican who moves from little group to little group, as they converse in low voices, no hysterics, no liquor. Some are slowly chewing on simple packed lunches. This older man carries an expensively acquired paunch and a gold watch. Is he the contractor who has brought the men here from Mexico? Do they pay him for the privilege of waiting for work like this? He has an amphibious sleekness. If he ever picked grapes it was a long time ago. He owns a small bus probably. That's how the men presumably got to the plaza in Healdsburg. It's a well-known pick-up point.

Where do these transients live during the harvest season? In sleeping bags somewhere? In trailers? What about their wives, their children? Back home in Mexico I guess. Waiting. Just like them. When the grape harvest is all done will they head back to those wives and kids? Or will they simply disappear into California's illegal immigrant community with the US Government's Immigration and Naturalization Service on their heels?

If California was a separate country instead of one state, out of all those others it would be the sixth richest country on the planet. No wonder the Mexicans come. They can earn maybe $8 (£4.60) or more an hour grape picking. There are, so I have learned, skilled tradesmen among them – carpenters, market gardeners, landscapers. The appeal of California for them is dramatically simple: they can earn as much in an hour here as in a day in Mexico. In a three month season of ten hour days, then, a man can earn enough to feed and clothe and entertain his family back in Oaxaca or wherever for eighteen months. The season, so I was told, finishes before Christmas time, when family duties call the intinerants back; besides, living in California through the dead season, at California prices, is no way to capitalise on months of labouring in vineyards.

RIGHT Kate Frey is comfortable on a pumpkin in Fetzer's organic garden, Hopland, Mendocino, which she supervises. It was the grapes from this garden which first alerted Fetzer's winemakers to the superior flavour of organic produce.

Some towns are doing more than merely tolerating casual seasonal labour. In the Russian River Valley is the hamlet of Graton. It has a large tractor showroom, a biggish pub, a tidy line of clapboard shops including a small supermarket and, as reported in *The Press Democrat*, the excellent local newspaper published in Santa Rosa, it has established a hiring hall, complete with toilet facilities, where "day labourers" can wait "off the streets and out of the weather". These day labourers have, so the paper said, been using "Graton's main street as a hiring hall for more than fifty years".

Mendocino
Understated elegance
This is California's most northern wine region and it's the hippiest. The politics are less sophisticated here, too. (A sign on one grape grower's premises, in Ukiah, reads: "Let's end this One World fiction! Get the United States out of the United Nations!") In Philo, the Navarro winery turns out Riesling, Pinot Gris, Gewurztraminer, and a chewily woody Pinot Noir. The wines show their cool-climate location in the Anderson Valley. This is also the location the Champagne house Roederer chose for its Californian operations and the bubblies here show how shrewd a choice this was: the wines are remarkably elegant and often finer in texture and subtlety and cleanness of expression than their distant cousins in Reims.

Hopland, however, is the place where the big action lies. So called for obvious reasons, Hopland has a soccer pitch but no hop vines any more; they've all been replaced by the grapes. Not a soul, not even the drinkers at the town's superbly lively micro-brewery bar (and the bewhiskered boozers at the dusty old Hells Angels bikers hang-out further along the main street), bemoans the fact. Hopland is where the Fetzer wine company operates, with many organic vineyards to its name, and the wines from here are largely well-priced, warmly-fruited, and widely available. Fetzer is the USA's organic wine pioneer.

Barney Fetzer began planting vineyards in 1958 and this was a family business for years. In 1992 it became part of the Brown-Forman empire. Today it is a big business, turning out three million cases a year (of which only a proportion are organic). Fetzer is one of the few wineries with its own in-house cooperage, and through this it has developed a deep understanding of wood and barrels.

At Fetzer there is also a part-time magician: Mr John Ash, consultant chef extraordinaire, who has an abundance of gob-smacking tricks – all done with the aid of a mirror (and only a little smoke from the stove). The mirror is some twenty feet long and is set at an angle above his head so that observers of his vegetarian cuisinery ("plant-based cooking" is his preferred term) can get a bird's eye view of the top of his head – no crown, but he could get away with one – and his cooking range. He stands behind it and struts his stuff and it is a sight to see.

CALIFORNIA

TOP Fetzer's Bonterra Muscat, in the handy half-bottle, reeks of grapes, tastes of grapes, and feels like satinised grape as it slides down.

BELOW LEFT John Ash takes lunch in Fetzer's organic garden with Bridget Harrington. Both teach cookery at Fetzer's school of cuisine. Two chefs eating their own food.

BELOW RIGHT It's not all done with mirrors (though there is smoke). The demonstration kitchen at Fetzer is designed so students and visitors can see everything.

His presentation style is an engrossing mixture of self-deprecation and hugely authoritative, healthy insight. "Don't ever use anything but sea-salt!" "Bell peppers are green and nutty, but best are these Mexican ones." "Do you realize it takes seven pounds of vegetable matter to produce one pound of cow?" This is all delivered with panache. His passions are flavour and natural ingredients, using vegetables and herbs in unpretentious combinations.

If Ralph Nader could break eggs and have Steve Martin's relaxed "but-I'm-really-in-control" kookiness, there you have the man called John Ash. He's a good vegetable-fearing Catholic in spirit and his food ideas should be turned into distillate and drip-fed to every American to drizzle over his/her food – all plant-based of course. With a food communicator this charismatic, this erudite, this visionary, and this important – especially when he's talking to ordinary Americans about revising their deadly ideas about carbohydrates and meat based diets – one can only be deeply impressed.

Kate Frey is also warm and friendly, and plant biased, and when it comes to discussing the advantages of organic gardening she's eloquent and technically highly informed. (In the picture, p.95, the pumpkin she is sitting on was grown purely for Halloween, but the vineyards behind her, being so liberally soaked, are not ornamental. Their grapes have been harvested and now they are being sown with seed crops between the vines to provide natural organic mulch for the vines. It was the Fetzer organic garden's grapes which first alerted the winemakers at Fetzer to the fact that the organic system, which forbids artificial fertilizers, pesticides, herbicides, and fungicides, could produce richer tasting fruit).

Kate is a great teacher and proselytiser of organic ways. Visitors who come and visit her two hectares of fruit trees, vegetables, herbs, flowers, and trees with their array of insects and birds (including the humming variety), go away with enriched minds. For my breakfast one morning I picked fresh russet apples and yellow cherry tomatoes.

Kate has changed things. When I first came here in the early 1990s there were no humming birds as there are now, and their arrival proves that organic methods not only benefit the drinker but other living creatures as well. Fetzer uses insect predators rather than pesticides to control the pests which plague grapes, and many vineyards throughout the world are now doing the same.

Wine writers are not universally loved in California. They tell a joke in Mendocino which sums up the general feeling. A famous wine writer dies and they have a collection to pay for the funeral. Wineries are asked to contribute $25 (£14.30) and everybody coughs up except one winemaker who eagerly hands over $50 (£28.70). "Here's fifty bucks," he says. "Why don't you bury two of them?"

A wise old Mendocino cellar hand defined his role in homely, down-to-earth terms which would horrify any Mondavist, anxious to maintain the mystique of winemaking as artistry. "Fruit naturally

ferments to become wine. The wine then wants to become vinegar and I'm in the middle, with the winemaker, somehow trying to lengthen the period between."

Bulldogs ahoy

All this crime you hear about in California, yet the only real threat to the person in up state Mendocino comes in the autumn as one walks the streets of Ukiah. The worst streets to walk are called Oak and Walnut. The assailants lurk in every tree. The acorns in particular being the nastiest as they descend and strike head or sidewalk or ricochet noisily off the parked vehicles. But Ukiah is a pleasant escape from Vinesville, as it has a couple of second-hand bookshops, two sushi bars, an excellent Thai restaurant (the Ruen Tong), a funky vacuum cleaner shop, a shop selling "Quality Firearms", two large antique emporia, and it has the marvellous, the inimitable, the coziest-of-cozy B&Bs The Sanford House (pictured left).

House guests can sit by the Koi carp pond in the Sanford House (corner of Stephenson and Pine) – in this town which calls itself the "number one small town in California" – and feed the fish from the plate of brownies left for you to help yourself. Smothering the gentle slurp of fish jaw are the occasional church bells. Every hour on the hour, in imitation of a band of slow but immaculately sequential campanologists, the church broadcasts (it cannot be said to peal) "Michael Rowed the Boat Shore, Allelujah!" It is, for the casual visitor, peculiarly comforting (and the carp don't seem bothered by it).

The Sanford House is also very friendly. The front door is often left unlocked. If the delightful owners have popped out, the guest finds a scribbled message prominently propped up on the table just inside the front door. It says: "To our guests: we've just popped out so make yourselves at home. Bob & Dorsey." You may wonder at such largesse, such confidence in the honesty of the neighbours, but when you see Guido, Bubba, and Spike, you feel that the house is safe against any alien invasion.

On the sofa in the living room lies Guido, the white bull dog. He knows I'm a guest by now. He turns to sniff at the brindle bulldog, Spike, who's reclining on a sofa reading *The San Francisco Chronicle* (he might just have been lying on it). The Boston terrier, Bubba, barks at me playfully and gestures, hopefully, in the direction of a red ball on the carpet. I'm forced to note that the smell of dog is not dissimilar to that of a badly tainted wine cork.

TOP Punching down the cap of Cabernet Sauvignon grape skins automatically saves a lot of manual labour (and gives the finished wine bite, depth, and tannic character). The wine style is, thus, wholly contrived by the winemaker.

BELOW The Fetzer cooperage at Hopland is attached to the winery. Rare anywhere in the world, in California it is unique.

RIGHT Tool of the trade. This one can shift grape residue while allowing the liquid wine to pass through unimpeded.

California's winemakers

MONTEREY COUNTY

CALERA
11300 Cienega Rd, Hollister, CA 95023
Tel: 831 637 9170. Fax: 831 637 9070
info@calerawine.com. www.calerawine.com
Winemaker: Josh Jensen

CHALONE
Stonewall Canyon Rd and Highway 146,
W. Soledad, CA 93960
Tel: 831 678 1717. Fax: 831 678 2742
chalone.vineyard.info@chalonevineyard.com
www.chalonevineyard.com
Winemaker: Dan Karlsen

ESTANCIA
1775 Metz road, Soledad, CA 93960
Tel: 707 967 2100. Fax: 707 967 2129
www.estanciaestates.com
Winemakers: Robert Cook, Chris Todd

JEKEL
40155 Walnut Ave, Greenfield, CA 93927
Tel: 674 5525. www.jekel.com
Winemaker: Cara Morrison

LOCKWOOD
59020 Paris Valley Rd, Salinas, CA 93902
Tel: 642 9200. info@lockwood-wine.com
www.lockwood-wine.com
Winemaker: Stephen Pessagno

J LOHR
1000 Lenzen Ave, San Jose, CA 95126
Tel: 408 288 5057. Fax: 408 993 2276
sjwinecenter@jlohr.com. www.jlohr.com
Winemaker: Jeff Meier

SMITH & HOOK
37700 Foothill Rd, Soledad, CA 93960
Tel: 831 678 2132. Fax: 831 678 2005
www2.ibgcheckout.com/smithhook
tastingroom@redshift.com
Winemaker: Art Nathan

TALBOTT
53 W. Carmel Valley Rd, Carmel Valley, CA
93924. Tel: 831 659 3500. Fax: 831 659 3515
www.talbottvineyards.com
Winemaker: Robert Talbott

VENTANA VINEYARD
Winery: 2999 Monterey-Salinas Highway,
Monterey, CA 93940. Tel: 831 372 7415
Fax: 831 375 0797. www.ventanawines.com
Winemaker: Doug Meador

LODI

LUCAS
18196 N Davis Road, Lodi, CA 95242
Tel: 209 368 2006. www.lucaswinery.com
Winemaker: David Lucas

MONDAVI WOODBRIDGE
5950 East Woodbridge Rd, Acampo, CA
95220. Tel: 209 369 5861
www.woodbridgewines.com
Winemaker: Brad Alderson

QUADY
13181 Road 24, Madera, CA 93639
Tel: 559 673 8068. Fax: 559 673 0744
info@quadywinery.com
www.quadywinery.com
Winemaker: Andrew Quady

SANTA CRUZ MOUNTAINS

AHLGREN
20320 Highway 9, Boulder Creek, CA 9500
Tel: 831 338 6071
ahlgren@ahlgrenvineyard.com
www.ahlgrenvineyard.com
Winemaker: Dexter Ahlgren

BARGETTO
3535 North Main St, Soquel, CA 95073
Tel: 831 475 2258. Fax: 831 475 2664
customerservice@bargetto.com
www.bargetto.com
Winemaker: Paul Wofford

BONNY DOON
10 Pine Flat Rd, Bonny Doon, CA 95060
Tel: 831 425 3625
www.bonnydoonvineyard.com
Winemaker: Randall Grahm

CINNABAR
23000 Congress Springs Rd, Saratoga,
CA 95070
Tel: 408 741 5858. Fax: 408 741 5860
cinnabarwine@yahoo.com
www.cinnabarwine.com
Winemaker: George Troquato

CRONIN
11 Old La Honda Rd, Woodside, CA 94062
Tel: 650 851 1452. Fax: 650 851 5696
Winemaker: Duane Cronin

DAVID BRUCE
21439 Bear Creek Rd, Los Gatos, CA
95030. Tel: 408 354 4214. Fax: 408 395 5478
DBW@davidbrucewinery.com
www.davidbrucewinery.com
Winemaker: David Bruce

HALLCREST
379 Felton Empire Rd, Felton, CA 95018
Tel: 831 355 4441. Fax: 831 335 4450
info@hallcrestvineyards.com
www.hallcrestvineyards.com
Winemaker: John Schumacher

KATHRYN KENNEDY
13180 Pierce Rd, Saratoga, CA 95070
Tel: 408 867 4170. Fax: 408 867 9463
cabernet@kathrynkennedywinery.com
www.kathrynkennedywinery.com
Winemaker: Marty Mathis

MOUNT EDEN
22020 Mount Eden Rd, Saratoga, CA 95070
Tel: 408 867 5832. info@mounteden.com
www.mounteden.com
Winemaker: Jeffrey Paterson

PAGE MILL WINERY
PO Box 2659, Livermore CA 94551
Tel: 925 456 7676. dane@pagemillwinery.com
www.pagemillwinery.com
Winemaker: Leopoldo Gonzalez

RIDGE
17100 Montebello Rd, Cupertino, CA
95015. Tel: 408 867 3233. Fax: 408 868 1350
wine@ridgewine.com. www.ridgewine.com
Winemaker: Paul Draper

SANTA CRUZ MOUNTAIN VINEYARD
2300 Jarvis Rd, Santa Cruz, CA 95065
Tel: 831 426 6209
Winemakers: Ken Burnap, Jeff Emery

THOMAS FOGARTY
5937 Alpine Rd, Portola Valley, CA 94028
Tel: 650 851 6777. Fax: 650 851 5840
info@fogartywinery.com
www.fogartywinery.com
Winemaker: Michael Martella

WOODSIDE VINEYARDS
340 Kings Mountain Rd, Carmel Valley,
CA 93924
Tel: 650 851 3144. Fax: 650 851 5037
info@woodsidevineyards.com
www.woodsidevineyards.com
Winemaker: Brian Caselden

SAN LUIS OBISPO COUNTY
TALLEY
3031 Lopez Dr, Arroyo Grande, CA 93420
Tel: 805 489 0446. Fax: 805 489 0996
info@talleyvineyards.com
www.talleyvineyards.com
Winemaker: Brian Talley

SANTA BARBARA COUNTY
AU BON CLIMAT
PO Box 113 Los Olivos, CA 93441
Tel: 805 937 9801. Fax: 805 937 2539
info@aubonclimat.com
www.aubonclimat.com
Winemaker: Jim Clendenen

CAMBRIA
5475 Chardonnay Lane, Santa Maria, CA
93454. Tel: 888 339 9463
info@cambriawines.com
www.cambriawines.com
Winemaker: David Guffy

FESS PARKER
6200 Foxen Canyon Rd, Los Olivos, CA
93441. Tel: 805 688 1545
www.fessparker.com
Winemaker: Eli Parker

QUPE
4665 Santa Maria Mesa Rd, Santa Maria,
CA 93454. Tel: 805 937 9801
Fax: 805 937 2539. Winemaker: Bob Lindquist

NAPA
ARAUJO
2155 Pickett Rd, Calistoga, CA 94515
Tel: 707 942 6061. Fax: 707 942 6471
wine@araujoestate.com
www.araujoestatewines.com
Winemaker: Francoise Pechon

CAKEBREAD
8300 St Helena Highway, Rutherford, CA
94573. Tel: 963 5221
cellars@cakebread.com
www.cakebread.com
Winemaker: Bruce Cakebread

CAYMUS
8700 Conn Creek Rd, Yountville, CA 94573
Tel: 707 963 4204. Fax: 707 963 5958
www.caymus.com
Winemaker: Chuck Wagner

CHATEAU MONTELENA
1429 Tubbs Lane, Calistoga, CA 94515
Tel: 707 942 5105. Fax: 707 942 4221
www.montelena.com
Winemaker: Bo Barrett

CLOS DU VAL
5330 Silverado Trail, Napa, CA 94558
Tel: 707 261 5200. Fax: 707 252 6125
cdv@closduval.com
www.closduval.com
Winemaker: Bernard Portet

CLOS PEGASE
1060 Dunaweal Lane, Calistoga, CA 94515
Tel: 707 942 4981. Fax: 707 942 4993
info@clospegase.com
www.clospegase.com
Winemaker: Bill Pease

CUVAISON
4550 Silverado Trail, Calistoga, CA 94515
Tel: 707 942 6266. Fax: 707 942 5732
www.cuvaison.com
Winemaker: John Thacher

DALLA VALLE
7776 Silverado Trail, Napa, CA 94558
Tel: 707 944 2676. Fax: 707 944 8411
info@dallavallevineyards.com
www.dallavallevineyards.com
Winemaker: Mia Klein

DARIOUSH
4240 Silverado Trail, Napa, CA 94558
Tel: 707 257 2345. Fax: 707 257 3132
www.darioushwinery.com
Winemaker: Steve Devitt

DIAMOND CREEK
1500 Diamond Mountain Rd, Calistoga,
CA 94515
Tel: 707 942 6926. Fax: 707 942 6936
www.diamondcreekvineyards.com
Winemaker: Al Brounstein

DOMINUS
POBox 3327, Yountville, CA 94599
Tel: 707 944 8954. Fax: 707 944 0547
info@dominusestate.com
www.dominusestate.com
Winemaker: Jean-Claude Berrouet

DUCKHORN
1000 Lodi Lane, St Helena, CA 94574
Tel: 707 963 7108
www.duckhornvineyards.com
Winemaker: Mark Beringer

FRANCISCAN
1178 Galleron Rd, Rutherford, CA 94573
Tel: 963 7111. www.franciscan.com
Winemaker: Larry Levin

FROG'S LEAP
8815 Conn Creek Rd, Rutherford, CA
94573. Tel: 707 963 4704. Fax: 707 963 0242
ribbit@frogsleap.com. www.frogsleap.com
Winemaker: John Williams

GRGICH HILLS CELLARS
1829 St Helena Highway, Rutherford, CA
94573. Tel: 963 2784. info@grgich.com
www.grgich.com. Winemaker: Mike Grgich

HARLAN ESTATE
POBox 352, Oakville, CA 94562
Tel: 707 944 1441. Fax: 707 944 1444
info@harlanestate.com
www.harlanestate.com
Winemaker: Bill Harlan

KENT RASMUSSEN
1001 Silverado Trail, St Helena, CA 94574
Tel: 707 963 5667
info@kentrasmussenwinery.com
www.kentrasmussenwinery.com
Winemaker: Kent Rasmussen

LOKOYA
7600 St Helena Highway, Oakville, CA
94562. Tel: 707 944 2807. Fax: 707 944 2824
lokoya.info@lokoya.com. www.lokoya.com
Winemaker: Marco DiGiulio

MAYACAMAS
1155 Lokoya Rd, Napa, CA 94558
Tel: 707 224 4030. Fax: 707 224 3979
mayacama@napanet.net
www.mayacamas.com
Winemaker: Bob Travers

MOUNT VEEDER
POBox 407, Rutherford, CA 94573
Tel: 963 7112. www.mtveeder.com
Winemaker: Larry Levin

NEWTON
2555 Madrona Ave, St Helena, CA 94574
Tel: 707 963 9000. Fax: 707 963 5408
winery@newtonvineyard.com
www.newtonvineyard.com
Winemaker: Peter Newton

NIEBAUM-COPPOLA
1991 St Helena Highway, Rutherford, CA
94573. Tel: 800 782 4266
www.niebaum-coppola.com
Winemaker: Francis Ford Coppola

OPUS ONE
7900 St Helena Highway, Oakville, CA
94562. Tel: 707 944 9442. Fax: 707 948 2497
Info@OpusOneWinery.com
www.opusonewinery.com
Winemakers: Patrick Leon, Tim Mondavi

PLUMPJACK
620 Oakville Crossroad, Napa, CA 94558
Tel: 707 945 1220. www.plumpjack.com
Winemaker: Nils Venge

ROBERT MONDAVI
7801 St Helena Highway, Oakville, CA
94562. Tel: 888 766 6328
info@robertmondaviwinery.com
www.robertmondavi.com
Winemakers: Bob & Tim Mondavi

SCREAMING EAGLE
POBox 134, Oakville, CA 94562
Tel: 707 944 0749. www.screamingeagle.com
Winemaker: Heidi Peterson Barrett

STAG'S LEAP WINE CELLARS
5766 Silverado Trail, Napa, CA 94558
Tel: 707 944 2020. Fax: 707 257 7501
www.cask23.com. Winemakers: Warren
Winiarski, John Gibson

STAGS' LEAP WINERY
6150 Silverado Trail, Napa, CA 94558
Tel: 707 944 1303
www.stagsleapwinery.com
Winemaker: Robert Brittan

SUTTER HOME
277 St Helena Highway, St Helena, CA
94574. Tel: 707 963 3104
www.sutterhome.com
Winemaker: Bob Trinchero

TURLEY WINE CELLARS
3358 St Helena Highway, St Helena, CA
94574. Tel: 707 963 0940
www.turleywinecellars.com
Winemaker: Ehren Jordan

SONOMA
ALEXANDER VALLEY VINEYARDS
8644 Highway 128, Healdsburg, CA 95448
Tel: 707 433 7209
avv@avvwine.com. www.avvwine.com
Winemaker: Hank Wetzel

ARROWOOD
14347 Highway 12, Glen Ellen, CA 95442
Tel: 707 935 2600. Fax: 707 938 5947
hospitality@arrowoodvineyards.com
www.arrowoodvineyards.com
Winemaker: Richard Arrowood

CLOS DU BOIS
19410 Geyersville Ave, Geyersville, CA
95441. Tel: 707 857 3100. Fax: 707 857 1667
cdb_wines@closdubois.com
www.closdubois.com
Winemaker: Frank Woods

CHATEAU ST JEAN
8555 Highway 12, Kenwood, CA 94542
Tel: 707 833 4134. www.chateaustjean.com
Winemaker: Steve Reeder

DELOACH
1791 Olivet Rd, Santa Rosa, CA 94501
Tel: 707 526 9111
winestore@deloachvineyards.com
www.deloachvineyards.com
Winemaker: Cecil DeLoach

DUXOUP
9611 West Dry Creek Rd, Healdsburg, CA
95448. Tel: 707 433 5195
www.duxoupwineworks.com
Winemaker: Andrew Cutter

FOPPIANO
12707 old Redwood Highway, Healdsburg,
CA 95448. Tel: 707 433 7272
Fax: 707 433 0565. louis@foppiano.com
www.foppiano.com. Winemaker: Bill Regan

HARTFORD COURT
8075 Martinelli Rd, Forestville, CA 95436
Tel: 707 887 1756. Fax: 707 887 7158
hartford.winery@hartfordwines.com
www.hartfordwines.com
Winemaker: Mike Sullivan

KENDALL-JACKSON
421 Aviation Blvd, Santa Rosa, CA 95403
Tel: 707 544 4000. kjwines@kj.com
www.kj.com. Winemaker: John Hawley

KISTLER
4707 Vine Hill RD, Sebastopol, CA 95472
Tel: 707 823 5603. Fax: 707 823 6709
info@kistlerwine.com. www.kistlerwine.com
Winemaker: Steve Kistler

LA CREMA
18700 Geyersville Ave, Geyersville, CA
95441. Tel: 800 314 1762. Fax: 707 571 1448
service@lacrema.com. www.lacrema.com
Winemakers: Michael & Anne Dashe

MARIMAR TORRES
11400 Graton Road, Sebastopol, CA 95472
Tel: 707 823 4365. Fax: 707 823 4496
info@marimarestate.com
www.marimarestate.com
Winemaker: Marimar Torres

MATANZAS CREEK
6097 Bennett Valley Rd, Santa Rosa, CA
95404. Tel: 707 528 6464. Fax: 707 571 0156
info@matanzascreek.com
www.matanzascreek.com
Winemakers: Susan Reed, Bill Parker

PEPI
see Other Wineries, Kendall-Jackson

PETER MICHAEL
12400 Ida Clayton Rd, Calistoga, CA 94515
Tel: 707 942 4459.
www.petermichaelwinery.com
Winemaker: Luc Morlet

RAVENSWOOD
18701 Gehricke Rd, Sonoma, CA 95476
Tel: 707 938 1960
rwwine@ravenswood-wine.com
www.ravenswood-wine.com
Winemaker: Joel Peterson

SIMI
16275 Healdsburg Ave, Healdsburg, CA
95448. Tel: 800 746 4880
information@simiwinery.com
www.simiwinery.com
Winemaker: Nick Goldschmidt

STONESTREET
4611 Thomas Rd, Healdsburg, CA 95448
Tel: 800 355 8008
info@stonestreetwines.com
www.stonestreetwines.com
Winemaker: Steve Teat

UNTI VINEYARDS
4202 Dry Creek Road, Healdsburg,
CA 95448. Tel: 707 433 5590
www.untivineyards.com
Winemakers: Mick Unti &
Sébastien Pochan

MENDOCINO COUNTY
EDMEADES
5500 Highway 128, Philo, CA 94566
Tel: 895 3232. info@edmeades.com
www.edmeades.com
Winemaker: Van Williamson

FETZER
12625 East Side Rd, Hopland, CA 95449
Tel: 707 744 7600. www.fetzer.com
Winemakers: Dennis Martin, Phil Hurst

NAVARRO
5601 Highway 128, Philo, CA 95466
Tel: 707 895 3686. Fax: 707 895 3647
www.navarrowine.com
Winemakers: Ted Bennett, Deborah Cahn

New Zealand

13 HOURS IN FRONT, 50 YEARS BEHIND.

"...the strong conviction that God had given them the finest climate... "

C V Smith, *A Humorous Survey of New Zealand* (1947).

Size may matter in all other walks of life, but not when it comes to wine. New Zealand has had a major impact on the world of wine, influencing both styles of fruit and vineyard. Yet in terms of its tonnage of wine grapes, the annual New Zealand wine harvest could be handled by one, just one, of the large southern French cooperatives.

The revolution in the world of wine is but two decades old and this stunning country has, every vintage, shown why it is a such an important vineyard nation. What began with Sauvignon Blanc and then Chardonnay, has moved to Pinot Noir, Pinot Gris, Viognier, and the international red varieties like Cabernet Sauvignon and Merlot. Gewurztraminer is also grown here, and several other varieties, and though it is Sauvignon Blanc which seems to excite most wine drinkers, with Pinot Noir providing thrills on the red side, there also some world class sparkling wines.

South Island
Four wine regions form the South's productive vineyard presence: Nelson; Marlborough; Canterbury; and Central Otago.

Central Otago
Severe elegance
This region is just about as south as you can get on the planet and still pick a wine grape. In such a climate Riesling is favoured, as is Pinot Noir (but Gewurztraminer, Chardonnay, and Sauvignon Blanc are not eschewed). It is, though, Pinot Noir which the growers pursue most ardently, in the fashion of their gold mining ancestors of the 1860s who opened up the territory (and planted vines there many decades before anyone thought of doing so in Marlborough). This dedicated pursuit – and the crick in the neck the growers acquire as a result of the firm nod they give Burgundy – characterizes these Pinots far more than any composition of vineyard soils.

Tasting all of Otago's Pinot Noirs side by side one gets a sense of a personality broadly common to each, which is surely a product of the similar outlooks and ambitions of the winemakers. The basis of the structure of each is black cherry and a tendency to a herbal, slightly green character in youth which, thanks to the excellent tannins (formed during those cold nights), offers the drinker the opportunity to age the wines for longer than other Kiwi Pinots – though not for many years.

The confidence of the modern Kiwi winemaker is well summed up by Otago (not Nuits-St-Georges) holding an annual Pinot Noir conference. One year a key-note speaker was the Londoner Anthony Hanson, an exquisitely urbane Christie's auctioneer and wine merchant with the manner of a retired psychiatrist to whom beautiful neurotic women still rush for expensive consolation. His role is to give delegates a run down of terroir in the Cote d'Or. Mr Hanson conjures up, via slides and charts, a breakdown of the viticultural real estate in this world-famous region.

PREVIOUS PAGE Before my first visit to New Zealand, the late Auberon Waugh said to me, "You'll love the country. It's like Britain in the fifties, only the girls are prettier." He was right about the girls but wrong about the rest. New Zealand's wine industry was, and is, hugely contemporary – even down to the design of its vineyards, as in the photograph on page 108. Note the carefully placed stones. Stones are precious to Marlborough's vineyard designers. They reflect the light up to the grapes, retain heat, and allow water to drain off.

RIGHT The ferry on Lake Wakatipu, Queenstown, is Edwardian with coal-fired boilers. New Zealanders have a great sense of tradition (so you don't get rid of something unless it no longer does the job and you have something much better with which to replace it).

But is the great man not a covert iconoclast? A man after my own heart? For after an hour of earthy remarks he says that if only Monsieur Gros's Clos de Vougeot had been made by Monsieur Bachelet of Gevrey-Chambertin, we would have got a different burgundy altogether.

Ah, so it's not terroir then. It's winemakers that create the differences. Does the audience appreciate this dynamic point, so subtly (and, perhaps, unintentionally) made?

Professor Warren Moran, academic Kiwi geographer, certainly does. He is the second key-note speaker and he talks about terroir from a different perspective. He is passionate, eloquent, committed, and a thorough no-bull academic.

Here are some of his soundbites, as he thoroughly demolishes the argument that terroir, as an expression of real estate, makes wines: "terroir is a marketing tool"; "we are part of nature and nature is part of us"; "people are involved with terroir"; and terroir "is a sum of many things". Then up comes a slide. It makes a convincing case which is summed up thus: "terroir is merely the expression of the process of winemaking." Then, also: "the vine is as complex as us." Finally, "vines define the essence of the place where they are grown but only taking into account "the human factors". If the factors change so does the terroir (and thus the wine)."

Small local Difficulty

The traveller embarks on a fantastically scenic and at times cutesily perfect rustic tour through the old gold-mining haven of Arrowtown to arrive at Mount Difficulty vineyards. This wine estate has one of the shrewdest names in NZ, let alone Central Otago, for it has the ring of confidence, like a certain toothpaste, which comes from its *insouciance*. Mount Difficulty just has to be an interesting wine, and indeed it is, being bottled in various manifestations of Pinot Noir, Pinot Gris, and Chardonnay. It is interesting to taste the four components of the Pinot Noir blend: Long Gully vineyard; Mansons Farms Vineyard; Target Gully Vineyard; and Pipeclay Terrace Vineyard. There is, in some snobbish quarters, a regard for single-vineyard wines. But blending them is the most creative opportunity the winemaker gets.

The world's most breathtaking vineyard?

To reach Rippon Vineyard one motors through intensely green, tufted valleys of stunning richness and elegance to reach the shores of Lake Wanaka. The stunning views make themselves clear beyond the vines, the mountains behind the lake forming an immense backdrop (making it a good choice as the location for the *Lord of the Rings* film trilogy).

Russell Lake, the man in charge of the vines, is a fund of carefully considered views – screwcaps, cork taint, terroir (about which, since he has worked in Burgundy, he has an opinion worth hearing). He pours scorn on geological fantasizing about wine. One tastes the superb wines made here – a gorgeously lean Riesling, as well as a decisive Pinot Noir – and muses that while Lake Wanaka undoubtedly influences the nature of the Rippon vines, of equal influence is surely Lake, Russell.

Of the other Otago producers, one can applaud the various stabs at Pinot Noir from Dry Gully's pleasant strawberry tones, to Olssens Slap Jack Creek's full-coloured richness. Quartz Reef's Pinot shows a fine, bitter cherry edge; Felton Road's the most tannic aplomb and finesse. Of this quartet, Felton Road seems to possess the tightest focus and ability to pick up character with bottle maturation.

Of other wineries, Carrick is far off Felton Road's accomplished style but for a winery which produced its first vintage only in 2000 shows great promise. Black Ridge, on the other hand, is one of the pioneers, having got going nearly twenty years before this, and its Pinot shows sedate cherry fruit with excellent tannins. Akarua's Pinot I found a little too juicy for me; Alexandra Wine Co's was dryer, nuttier, more stylish. This leaves two exemplars of the Otago style with the world's most neurotic grape: Chard Farm and Gibbston Valley.

Chard Farm's Reserve Pinot Noir can be a well-tailored specimen, with its touch of sweetness held by calm tannins and level-headed raspberry and cherry fruit. For me, though, it was the Gibbston Valley Pinot which set a standard for richness and elegance (certainly in the 2000 vintage) that few other local producers bettered, though Mount Difficulty and Two Paddocks were up there with it and have later vintages they can claim as pertinent if not superior.

Central Otago is a small community of wine producers committed to calming the neuroses of the Pinot Noir grape without lapsing into the genteel obsessive madness which can possess some producers of it (from Romania to South Africa). Apart from Riesling, no other grape breeds such fanatical producers – the other difference is that with the latter grape you can make a half-decent wine more easily. With Pinot Noir you sweat blood. Perhaps that accounts for the gamier flavour of the most sensual examples.

Light not-so-fantastic

The extraordinary intensity of UV light in NZ, caused by deterioration of the earth's ozone layer in the biosphere directly over the country, is a factor, hitherto hardly discussed, of the grapes' development. Does this light dramatically affect NZ's vines' physiological development? By opening up grape canopies – a viticultural technique developed in New Zealand – this light can be even more concentrated because leaf cover is less in such vineyards. Is this the reason many New Zealand wines do not age especially brilliantly? Are grape phenolics, which in other wines produce tannins and acids making possible years of potential bottle ageing, more fragile in NZ wines? Kevin Judd at Cloudy Bay once said to me: "Why can't we make wines which last in New Zealand?" and he produced a middle-aged sweet white wine which was already the colour

TOP Rippon Vineyard on Lake Wanaka is reckoned by romantics to be the most dramatically situated in the world. But it's the wine that matters and it can be outstanding (because of another Lake, Russell Lake, the winemaker).

BELOW Napier has an abundance of art deco buildings. The National Tobacco Company's HQ, built in 1933, was designed by local resident architect Louis Hay.

RIGHT-HAND PAGE

TOP Stonybridge Vineyard boasts designer wines from very fecund vines.

CENTRE LEFT The wine from Te Motu vineyard is a family affair: the Dunleavys run the estate together, father Terry and sons John and Paul.

CENTRE RIGHT Tony Forsyth of Te Whau vineyards (pictured) smiles regularly at his vines. Herb Friedli, who turns the grapes into wine, is less flamboyant (and the liquids show both men's characters).

BELOW LEFT Who needs a spectacular view of Queenstown when you can enjoy a view of a spectacular local Pinot Noir (Felton Road)?

BELOW RIGHT Villa Maria screwcaps every wine it produces. Owner and MD, George Fistonich, is New Zealand's most influential wine businessman.

LEFT Judy and Tim Finn of Neudorf vineyards, Nelson, not only introduced me to their stunning tomatoes, their stunning Sauvignon Blancs and Pinot Noirs, but to the stunning writing of Owen Marshall (far right on p.117).

RIGHT The Finns swear by screwcaps.

of brown ale and had acids prodigiously advanced. It looked and smelled like it was thirty years old not the eight or nine it was.

Geisenheim wine university, on the Rhine, is now taking the theory seriously, and is engaged on a scientific investigation of the effect UV light has on wine grapes.

Waipara
No muddy water in sight

At Pegasus Bay, the winery situated further north from the Canterbury Plain in Waipara, we meet the delightful Ivan Donaldson, neurosurgeon, winery proprietor, all-round good egg. He and I once sat opposite one another for several days in the Blue Mountains in Sydney tasting wines with food. We were both judges at the Sydney 100 International Wine Competition. He stood up to the madnesses of the judging procedures very well, but I folded on the last morning (around 9am) faced with a steaming kangaroo pie and thirty-eight bottles of Shiraz. Of his own wine, a Pinot Noir, which we sampled one evening, he was frank and unassuming when asked how the wine might have fared had it been entered in the competition. "We'd have thrown the bloody thing out," he responded acidly (a somewhat harsh judgement on a wine which in vintages other than the one tasted would, I am sure, show itself to be as good as any other local specimen).

The Pinot Noir made by Danny Schuster at Omihi Hills in Waipara would not be thrown out of any competition. Danny goes in for a wonderfully structured artefact, boldly scented, gamey and old-fashionedly Burgundian in temperament, and its headiness is such that it has even seduced Pinotphiles like Michel Roux junior, the chef at

LEFT They are partial to felines at Cooper's Creek winery.

RIGHT Owen Marshall is one of the world's most delicious short-story writers. He lives in Timaru, which Bill Bryson scandalously described as the most boring town in New Zealand.

London's distinguished Michelin three-star restaurant, Le Gavroche. Serving up a dish of red mullet with ceps and red wine sauce, Michel insisted this was the wine to drink and he was right. The delicate fish was not overwhelmed and the wild mushrooms were enhanced by the wine's quite beautiful perfume and wild-raspberry undertone.

Nelson
Finnland
Nelson is a small area of some dozen producers, the most well known being Neudorf and Seifreid Estate. The area is only seventy-five kilometres (121 miles) from Marlborough, but the two areas, each with its principal town (Marlborough's being Blenheim), could not be more different. Nelson is a "tairrably naice" small seaside town, the roundabouts are very charming and abundantly green and the locals give way to you.

Tim and Judy Finn, of Neudorf Estate, are one of the most respected and admired wine producing teams in the country. Neudorf produces some of the most subtly beautiful Sauvignons and Chardonnays in the world. Its Pinot is fast catching up (especially now it's been screwcapped).

With the vineyards a few feet away, and the sounds of the bird-scarer gas guns peppering the conversation, Tim presents his wines. The Neudorf Nelson Chardonnay, whole bunch pressed and made using wild yeast, is a glycerol-coated marvel of gorgeous, slightly smoky fruit. "It was pretty funky to start off with," says Tim: "Some odd organisms there, but the wine has settled down perfectly in bottle." Next is a wine made from contract grapes grown in Marlborough, a Sauvignon. I found it straightforward, as these things go in Marlborough, with a tropical fruit undertone. "I find it has a slight tree quality. From the cork," says Tim.

TOP One of the less beautiful aspects of many Kiwi vineyards is the netting put up to frustrate the local avian population which knows a ripe grape when it sees one.

BELOW LEFT Rosemary and Brent Marris of Wither Hills vineyards, Marlborough, on holiday in Noosa Heads, Queensland, Australia. Brent's versatility across many wine styles, red and white, is unsurpassed.

BELOW RIGHT Kevin Judd makes Cloudy Bay, NZ's most iconic Sauvignon Blanc and Chardonnay. The estate also turns out Pelorus, a masterpiece of emphatic delicacy in sparkling wine.

Then Tim produces his speciality Pinot Noir, two bottles of the same 2001 wine, one screwcapped, the other sealed with a cork. The wine had been in bottle exactly two months. The screwcapped example has a lovely opulent style, with no sweetness or soppiness. It parades plums, cherries, a hint of tarry glycerol, soft, well integrated tannins with a faint toffee edge. It's lovely wine. The same wine under its cork already shows the oxidative effects of aspiration through the cork. The wine is less compacted than the first. In a year, there would be an even more dramatic difference between the wines. I daresay the one under cork would struggle to last five or six years with its fruit in fine condition.

In 2005, two examples of these 2001 Pinots were tasted again. The one sealed with a cork was more advanced aromatically, not surprisingly, but the screwcapped example was far superior in flavour and texture. It had developed a subtle spiciness, like Lapsang tea, and its tannins were tight and beautifully sleek.

Herman Seifried makes wines in total contrast to the Finns. Herman is built like a Springbok front row forward. He even sounds like a Springbok front row forward. His wines are similarly broad and muscular and they wrestle the palate to the ground; you either submit or struggle. I found myself tasting Sauvignons, Gewurztraminers, Rieslings, Chardonnays, Pinot Noirs, and Merlots, and feeling somewhat daunted by the bullishness of the fruit.

Why are Kiwis so keen on screwcaps? Because they get letters from their cork suppliers saying this: "Cork is not neutral in flavour, it has a soft wood flavour characteristic. 2-4-6 Trichloranisole (TCA), an environmental pollutant, is found to contaminate many corks. Until a method of eliminating TCA in cork is discovered we cannot warrant our supply as TCA free." Would any sane individual put such a product in touch with his or her wine in these circumstances? Yet TCA is not cork's greatest weakness. The biggest problem with cork is that its permeability causes variation, so that bottles of any wine laid down to age will mature differently, often dramatically so, and so be wildly inconsistent.

Marlborough
From millions of apples to millions of dollars
Brent Marris's winemaking ingenuities were long evident when he worked for Delegat's, but then he went into partnership with his dad Mike, and Mike's old apple orchards became vineyards. And then Lion-Nathan, the big alcohol conglomerate came along and said, we like the look of this, and Marris, *pere et fils*, shook hands on a deal. And the results are stunning. The family has millions in the bank, Lion-Nathan owns Wither Hills, and we still get masses of character and style in the bottle. The winery, built around the old apple packing plant, now distinguishes Wither Hills with its 120 hectares of vines as a leading Marlborough producer (with another 120 hectares waiting to come into production).

119

"In 1973," says Mike, "we were just a little country town… now…" In 1973 you could buy an acre of land with water rights for NZ$250 (£95). By 2000 you wouldn't pay less than NZ$30,000 (£11,350) and maybe as much as NZ $40,000 (£15,150). Since then it's gone beyond NZ$50,000 (£19,000). It's not exactly gold rush time in Marlborough, but it is gold amble.

Small earthquake in wine bottle

It is impossible to underdramatise the impact of Cloudy Bay, not only on the British market, but also the world wine scene. When, in 1986, the ethereally labelled white wine claiming to be authentic Sauvignon Blanc and called Cloudy Bay arrived in the UK, aficionados were struck by the elegance of this labelling, but expected nothing more than the usual not-a-bad-stab-but-nothing-like-the-real-thing sort of liquid. However, the liquid turned out not only to be sensational, but sensationally concentrated, pure, gorgeous Sauvignon, and it reminded certain old soaks of the grape as it had once been fashioned by the vignerons of Sancerre.

Today, even the French acknowledge Marlborough's superiority with the grape. Henri Bourgeois, Sancerre doyen, has pitched up here and bought vineyard land. He threw a party at which he invited all the locals of note (i.e. everyone) and said: "We have come here to learn from you, not the other way round."

It is not only Cloudy Bay's Sauvignon that can be exquisite (though many other Marlborough Sauvignons rival it and in some vintages are more biting). Pelorus, the winery's sparkling wine, is superbly elegant yet emphatic, with a luxurious undertone, yet it's a third, sometimes a fifth, of the price of comparable Champagnes. Cloudy Bay Chardonnay is also shapely, along with a rarely seen Gewurztraminer. The late harvest Riesling, given five or six years of bottle age, can be extraordinary (the additional grape sugars in the wine help it live longer). Also provocative, if a difficult ascent, and scent, for the nose, is a wine from Cloudy Bay called Te Koko, a Sauvignon Blanc which is winemaker Kevin Judd's experiment with wild yeast. The urge to experiment here in NZ is more prevalent than in established wine estates in the Old World. The word "established" is relative, I suppose, but amongst the myriad Marlborough parvenus, Cloudy Bay does carry the air of a grand seigneur.

A Stitch in time

John and Jo Stitchbury run and own Jackson Estate and live in a home counties-style house of the sort within which Agatha Christie villains meet their nemeses. There is, then, little of modern New Zealand evoked therein except from the estate's palatable Sauvignon Blanc, Chardonnay, and Pinot Noir.

John himself has his eccentricities. In order to read one wine label, having lost his reading glasses, he picks up an old oculist's box of lenses and fiddles around with the eye-testing spectacle frame, inserting lens after lens, until he finds the prescription which suit his eyes. For this gifted engineer, life is a giant box of toys always open and ready to be assembled and disassembled. He sleeps with a weather station alarm by his bed in winter, connected to a sensory system in the vineyard, so he knows instantly if there's going to be a frost (at which point up goes the local helicopter to drive warm air down to the vines).

Mike and Claire Allan of Huia (pronounced who-ya, the Maori name for some kind of bird) produce a bunch of wines which are remarkably individual, consistently delicious, and superbly well structured. The sparkling Chardonnay/Pinot Noir has subtle minerals with peaches and cream richness which is not OTT. The Sauvignon Blanc is concentrated with gentle tropicality. The Riesling offers lime with underripe gooseberry. The Pinot Gris has a beautiful texture. The Gewurztraminer is fabulously complete. The Chardonnay is erotic. The Pinot Noir dynamic.

"We do a small amount of whole bunch pressing here, which is a bit controversial among wine growers... and that's where that silky texture you keep remarking on comes from," says Mike.

They also use wild rather than commercial yeasts, which give more glycerol and grip to the fruit on the mid-palate. The wines achieve individuality and balance without struggle; they have class. They are complex and bold; have great finesse and style. Huia is a real find, a true gem, with a wit running through everything it does – and not just with the wines. The winery is a *bijou* miracle and even the small public tasting room is a tribute to good taste: design flair without showiness.

At Nautilus winemaker Clive Jones offers the adventurous palate some fairly gripping wines: Sparkling Brut (crisp with lemon and raspberry), Chardonnay (gooseberry and fresh lemon), Pinot Gris (apricot and lime), Sauvignon Blanc (tangy with a real zing on the finish), and a very fleshy Pinot Noir.

Marlborough has many places to wine and dine well, but at chez Scott (Allan and Cathy) I had the chance to savour some old bottles. The family house, compact and stylish, is a bungalow, but elder Allan Scott wines work on many levels. A ten-year-old Riesling drunk here over supper is beguiling – taut, oily, rich yet elegant.

Lawson's Dry Hills

Ross and Barbara Lawson have their compact winery in Marlborough's Alabama Road, in front of the parched-looking Wither Hills, and they make there a range of wines which has been highly individual and compelling since 1992. A challenging yet delicious experience it is to taste this range (even the Pinot rosé has lovely dry cherry fruit). The Sauvignon Blanc is gorgeously smooth, never clumsily herbaceous. The Pinot Gris shows a remarkable concentration of dry apricot. The Chardonnay is rich and creamy in warm vintages, more citrousy in cooler ones. The Gewurztraminer is invariably clotted and pungent. The Riesling, with age, goes petrolly and classic. The Pinot Noir, ah, well, the Pinot Noir can be a bit juicy. The Late Harvest Semillon is highly

concentrated. The Late Harvest Riesling is beautifully textured. Ross Lawson sheared sheep and built swimming pools before he got into the winery business. With Barbara and Dry Hills he has dug a little goldmine.

In the Forrest something stirs

And what stirs is a passion for screwcaps. John Forrest is a pioneer for this sealing method as far as Marlborough is concerned, and going through various specimens of his wines, some screwcapped, some with corks, one appreciates why. The Sauvignon Blancs are patently fresher and more concentrated in a screwcap and so are several Rieslings. The rosé is firm and tightly focussed. His Chardonnay is a classic specimen of Marlborough elegance, but the screwcapped Gewurztraminer is simply sublime, richly endowed with Turkish delight fruit and excellent acid structure. How come his Sauvignon has such pungency and aroma? "Little secret," he confides: "In a cool year I'll add 2–4 per cent Riesling."

The tasting finishes with a lovely Pinot Noir, a terrific Chenin Blanc Late Harvest (it's like an exotic Quarts de Chaume, the great Loire sweet white), and an exquisite Botrytized Riesling. I also taste John's reds made in Hawkes Bay in the North Island and these Cabernets and Merlots show great tannins. Also remarkable are the rich tannins in his Pinot Noirs.

"Ah! Pinot Noir," he exclaims. "It helps to be a bloody minded academic to make great Pinot."

Rod at the ready

Hitch a ride with David Pearce of Grove Mill and you become aware of a rod and line already hooked and lured up in the back of his station wagon. It is not there for decoration. This man is a serious trout and salmon catcher and if he feels the office or the wines (he is Grove Mills' maker of such things) are getting on top of him, he dons his yellow wellies and gets into the nearest stream – of which Marlborough has several bursting with gullible fish – for a short break.

Grove Mill's wines, in similar fashion, have caught the imagination of drinkers who can spot a bargain when it's under their noses. Frog Haven Pinot Gris drips with succulent apricot and pineapple. Grove Mill Sauvignon Blanc has a multiple thwack of pineapple, melon, lemon, and lime. Grove Mill Chardonnay has tropical mango with pineapple. Grove Mill Riesling also has a touch of mango with a lemon zestiness. Grove Mill Pinot Gris flaunts rich marshmallow fruit, superb to partner with complex fish dishes. Grove Mill Pinot Noir shows liquorice and cobnut with soft tannins.

A dinner of sublimely succulent, lightly gamey, local scallops at Marlborough's Hotel d'Urville, with a bottle of seven-year-old Hunter's Riesling, proves to be one of the highlights of my gastronomic career thus far on this planet. Why is it that New Zealand whites can mature with such greater elegance than the reds? Is the shortness of life of the reds due to the UV light affecting the antioxidant tannins in the grape skins?

The richly loving relationship a man may have with his vines (and his wife with his laundry)

Isabel Estate is named after Michael Tiller's mother. Mr Tiller is a deeply sentimental individual. Michael met his wife Robyn when she was "an air hostess", and he was an ANZ pilot. Robyn told me she often has to remove little wire cane-ties from Michael's pockets before dumping his dirty clothes in the washing machine. The ex-airline pilot has the habit, on his walk to work through the vineyard each morning from the family house to the winery, of checking on his vines and retying any canes which may not be as neatly tied up as they might be. "Once," says Robyn, with a tender sigh, "I nearly threw a pair of his trousers with secateurs in the back pocket into the machine." Such is the richly loving relationship a man may have with his vines and his wife with his laundry.

And, as a result, the wines are soft and approachable also. Isabel Estate's range of Sauvignon Blanc, Riesling, Chardonnay, Pinot Gris, Pinot Noir, and a remarkable sweet wine called Noble Sauvage is light, undemanding, charming.

Highfield Estate is owned by Tom Tenuwera, a Bath-based Sri Lankan businessman, and Shin Yokoi of Osaka. Is this, then, an estate which is merely a richman's toy? Not when one tastes Estree Sparkling Brut, made with the help of Champagne consultant Michel Drappier. The wine is remarkably subtle and dry and I'd defy anyone, given a bottle a few years of age, not to confuse it with a mature Bollinger. The Riesling, Sauvignon Blanc, Chardonnay, and Pinot Noir are not quite capable of inspiring such an encomium. The Chardonnay comes pretty close to having a classic French profile, so it needs to shed that if it's to become a signed-up New World hipster. In spite of its lemon and pineapple tang it reminded me of a slightly quirky Meursault.

We're only Number One so we try harder

Touring the Montana company's new Awatere vineyards only emphasises just how growth-minded New Zealand's largest wine producer is. This ambitious project increases Montana's share of New Zealand's vineyard planting (now more than 15,000 hectares out of the country's total of 20,500) and confirms its position as the country's largest producer by a considerable margin. Indeed, Montana produces seventy per cent of the country's wines. But let us not forget that this is a very small country, with fewer inhabitants than some English counties (4 million). There are less than 400 wine producers (plus around 600 growers) and by producing 150,000 tonnes of wine grapes in a good year they place NZ at about the same productive capacity as a couple of large Languedoc wine co-ops.

Large or not, Montana is equally as sentimental as most wine producers here. The Marlborough winery's hospitality area has an old-fashioned feel, including a concert Steinway acquired as part of Montana's interest in encouraging classical music. The piano once

RIGHT Therese Herzog, front of house, runs New Zealand's crispest hotel restaurant. Husband Hans, back of winery, conjures magical, meticulous, mouth-enhancing liquids to match the food from his own organic vines nearby: Chardonnay, Viognier, Pinot Noir, Cabernet Sauvignon, Merlot, Cabernet Franc, and Malbec. The yields are low: a bottle per vine.

MARLBOROUGH

belonged to Rachmaninov, apparently. There is a suitably classical feel to most of the company's wines, with the most melodic being the Sauvignon Blanc and the Riesling. Occasionally a Pinot Noir appears which is a thumping bargain also. For many drinkers, Montana is their first taste of New Zealand wine and it seems to me the company takes that responsibility seriously and does not rest idly on its laurels.

Such niceties as laurel-resting do not, however, trouble the commercial horizons of Marlborough's quaintest winery: Johanneshof Cellars. Owned and run by Warwick Foley and Edel Everling, this tiny producer has the only cellar built into rock, German-style, in the region. Its wines are solidly, marvellously, deliciously individual. Edel explains the world of Johanneshof: "When Jim Bulger was prime minister," she begins, "he visited our cellar and said you can't drink out of these old bottles can you? They're all covered in mould. They're so old. Can you drink wine old?"

They make gripping wines here: a stunning Riesling, a done-to-a-crisp Sauvignon Blanc, a satiny Chardonnay, a lightly pungent Pinot Noir, a pert Pinot Gris, and a fresh Sekt-like Emmi Sparkling wine. If nothing else, Johanneshof seems to be able to make wines which can age well. It uses some wild yeasts here, which means that the usual inoculation habits of NZ winemakers are not routinely followed. The result is some entertaining, if not always complete, wines.

An unadulterated paradise of the sort usually found only in Lyon or Strasbourg
Herzog's does not promise much from the outside. Shrubs flutter in the breeze, flowers beam benignly; the restaurant's building might be a headmistress's sea-side retirement home. Smug vineyards surround it.

Upon entry, however, another world beckons. It is the world where Michelin food guide inspectors climb the oxygenated highest peaks to assess the talents of monastic chefs and the contents of commodious wine cellars. Immaculately laid tables and starched linen table cloths reflect only the superficialities of a serious eatery. Herzog's chef Louis Schindler's cooking resolutely puts the kitchen in the *trois etoiles* category. If this is not the finest restaurant in New Zealand I am Rachel Hunter.

Therese Herzog, front of house, introduces her husband Hans. In his shy way, in the reserved manner of someone from German-speaking Switzerland who has had to imbibe English from the polished floor up, it slowly becomes apparent that the vines outside are his. Hans Herzog makes wines. Indeed, the sensitive taster is quickly made aware as s/he tastes that no-one is making better wine in the whole of New Zealand than Hans Herzog.

He uses wild yeasts, that is to say the yeasts nature has deposited on the skins of the grapes and wafted around the winery. His vines, on just twelve hectares, receive no chemical fertilizers, fungicides, or pesticides. His yields are low ("one bottle of wine per vine", he tells me). He does not leaf pluck his vines, so they have natural shelter from the cruel UV light. His methods are traditional, old-fashioned, and representative of pure committed craftsmanship. His luscious liquids are as good, if not better, than anything that has ever passed my lips as great New Zealand wine.

Herzog Chardonnay is composed of complex, smoky melon and a touch of soft fruit. I rated the 2001 19 points out of 20. The Viognier has classic apricot richness and will age beautifully. The Pinot Noir has fine tannins and dark cherry fruit. His "Montepulciano" is so stunningly concentrated as to make one choke with pleasure. The Bordeaux blend – Merlot, Cabernet Sauvignon, Cabernet Franc, and Malbec – offers liquorice, nuts, fine-toned berries, and smooth tannic power.

Eye for an angle, nose for a vine

Michael Seresin is an international cine-photographer and filmmaker who decided he needed a serious hobby. To turn his grapes into wine he turned to Brian Bicknell, whose approach I am thoroughly intimate with from the many lush and lissom wines he turned out for Errázuriz in Chile. Mike lured him back to their jointly native New Zealand.

The wines here are beautiful. A terrific Pinot Gris, a lovely Chardonnay, an exciting Chardonnay Reserve, an arousingly tannic Pinot Noir (which has a subtle liquorice richness). Brian prompts interesting dialogue over two Sauvignons from the same tank, both bottled 13th September 2001. But one bottle sports a cork, the other a screwcap. The latter wine simply leaps out of the glass. The cork stoppered wine is much duller.

Said Brian: "At first, the wine sealed with a cork seemed better, for a month or so after bottling. But it became apparent that the screwcapped wine stayed fresher. It was more true to the wine in the tank. The wine I'd made. The cork was affecting the acids."

North Island

In terms of wine areas here you find, from north to south: Matakana; Kumei/Huapai; Waiheke Island; Henderson; Waikato; Gisborne; Hawkes Bay; and Wairarapa.

Martinborough
Boutique or department store?

Martinborough's town centre has become like a tasteful outdoor shopping mall. It has *bijou* shops and eating places and it boasts the spiffingly good Martinborough Hotel which, on my first visit to the town years back, was a spit and sawdust pub I was advised to steer clear of. Could it have been a hangout of violent characters? Unlikely. The nearest thing to physical violence in this township is when a farmer raises his voice to a sheep: "Hey, ewe, yes, ewe!"

But it is a happening location with regard to wine. Palliser is a well-known name, exporting energetically. The Pinot Noirs show good tannic grip. The Riesling is a bit of a Mae West (fat and unsubtle). The Pinot Gris drips with delicious apricot. The Sauvignon Blanc is concentrated. The Pencarrow Chardonnay is very American oaky which peels away to reveal some crisp tanginess. The Palliser Estate Chardonnay is subtle, complex, delicious. The Pinot Noir seems stripped of tannins.

Richard Riddiford, Palliser's managing director, has screwcaps statistically evaluated: "I know," he says, "that I'll have 30,000 bottles of wine a year which have been affected by cork taint, 18,000 of them very obviously. We get less than twelve bottles a year returned in that time. Yet we have a clear policy of replacing corked bottles. So I deduce that people either don't notice the taint or, in many cases, don't like the wine and never buy our product again. What other luxury item in the world would put up with a guaranteed ten per cent failure rate? We'll go over to screwcaps 100 per cent."

Pioneering with Pinot

Martinborough Vineyard is the winery operation that pioneered Pinot Noir in this area. The vineyard is the result of a report, carried out in the late 1970s, that analysed which of New Zealand's regions were the most appropriate for growing wine grapes – particularly the so-called "classic" varieties. This report apparently concluded that Martinborough was not dissimilar to Burgundy in regional climatic profile. However, the most exciting wine here is not Pinot Noir but Pinot Gris (not found in Burgundy but Alsace).

Executive Chairman of the company, Duncan Milne, wishing to contradict my assertion that Kiwi Pinots cannot age and therefore cannot exhibit Burgundian characteristics, opened in February 2002, a 1994, a 1995, and a 1996 reserve. Only this last, to my palate, had any living structure worth remarking on.

TOP The township of Martinborough is not large, but the hotel is unmissable. Restored and extended in 1996 from its 1882 birth as a hostelry, it offers luxury without ceremony.

BELOW LEFT Beer and wine don't mix? Tell that to Beer, the dog, and to anyone at Palliser Estate where the animal, a trifle listlessly, hangs out.

BELOW RIGHT Alana Estate is named after the beauty on the right. The beauty on the left is her husband, Ian. Mr and Mrs Smart, who have been producing wine since 1995, lived up to their name when they settled in Martinborough to produce wine.

TOP With the Nga Waka-a-Kupe Hills in the background Steve Smith and Peter Wilkins, of Craggy Range, look the part of pioneers (which they are, as the vineyards behind were sheep paddocks only yesteryear).

CENTRE LEFT Claire Mulholland of Martinborough Vineyards brings some style to racking barrels.

CENTRE RIGHT The sun always shines in Hawke's Bay? Nope.

BELOW The town of Napier (totally rebuilt in 1931 after a 7.8 Richter scale earthquake) is a monument to Art Deco architecture. It makes a fitting complement to the local Hawkes Bay Cabernets and Merlots, themselves full of neat angles.

Schubert in C-major

Kai Schubert and Marion Deimling are German romantics. "We had been looking," Kai says, "for an ideal area to grow premium Pinot Noir for quite a while. We searched in several countries, Oregon, California, Australia, and France, but in the end the Wairarapa in New Zealand, here in Martinborough, was the most interesting region to us."

"In autumn 1998," he goes on, "we acquired a small, established vineyard in Martinborough and about sixteen hectares of bare land. On the land we planted twelve hectares of vines, three-quarters Pinot Noir. We've planted other varieties and we have grapes grown under contract over in Hawkes Bay."

However, Pinot is his passion and it shows in his 2003 (touching £20 in the UK, rating 17.5 points out of 20). Tasted in 2005, it was a sleek, complete Pinot Noir experience from nose to throat. It had simply gorgeous, gamey, black cherry fruit with leafy tannins and a texture of satin ruffled by taffeta. It was, in short, Kai Schubert vinified and poured into a wine bottle.

A morning pluck

At Te Kairanga, Andrew Shackleton, the chief executive, and Peter Caldwell, the winemaker, are effusive proponents of Martinborough and the finesse they believe is its hallmark. "We're looking," says Andrew, "for refinement in the reserve wines. Nothing OTT. Wines which will open up in the mouth and cellar well for two or three years."

He confirms they leaf pluck but "only on the morning side", which is an interesting idea. This way, the grapes will get a good dose of early sun before it moves round and the day gets hot. But this technique takes no account of UV light.

A nine year-old Pinot Noir, from my notes, showed no great willingness to age gracefully: "Cabbagey aroma, breakdown of glycerol, tannin lack, fruit withered." Andrew, on the other hand, believes it is "still holding up well".

Ata Rangi – moment of truth

The best Martinborough wine I have ever tasted came from this organic estate. Winemaker Clive Paton took me to his cellar and poured me something called Celebre, a blend of Shiraz and Cabernets Sauvignon and Franc. It exploded on the palate.

Dry River

Joelle Thompson, New Zealand's least stuffy wine writer, once invited me to join her for lunch in Auckland at Sausalito in Northcote Point. She brought along Dry River Riesling 2001 and Dry River Pinot Noir 1996. Both wines were glorious, but the red drew from me the exultation: "Eureka! A Martinborough Pinot which smells of Pinot!" What was left of the Riesling, from a three-quarters finished bottle, still managed to be an

MARTINBOROUGH

130

accomplished liquid two days later. Dry River's winemaker, Neil McCallum, I was told, goes in for reflective mulching, a policy which helps his vines to produce such interesting, complex wines. It is not a subject, reflective mulching, you should enquire too deeply into; the gory details are too sensational for publication.

Hawkes Bay

Where there's muck there's brass. Where's there a lot of muck....
Craggy Range is owned by Terry Peabody, a US businessman involved in waste management and truck manufacture and he is loaded. This benign enthusiast for things which grow in New Zealand has pumped NZ$50 million (£19 million) into the Craggy Range vineyards and winery, and the man who oversees it all is minority shareholder and viticulturalist Steve Smith – whose dynamism is inexhaustible, passion limitless. The company owns a massive 800 hectares of land in Hawkes Bay, on the so-called Gimblett Gravels, but it has also planted vines near Martinborough, beneath the Nga Waka-a-Kupe Hills. This is a little way out of the town but still, Steve insists (though purists, and indeed future geographers, may demur), "part of Martinborough" and enjoying that appellation.

The hills name means The Canoes of Kupe and refers to the Maori legend of Kupe, the god who fished up North Island. He beached his canoes here to be overgrown into these hills. There is nothing in this legend which does not find equal resonance in some of the fantastic wine legends of Burgundy or Bordeaux or Champagne.

Peter Wilkins, who manages the Nga Waka-a-Kupe vines, says "We'll be organic within five years."

"And," says Steve, "we'll get 300 tonnes of hand-picked Pinot Noir off this land and build a winery here." He points to a large triangular depression in the ground which will form the basis of the barrel cellar. Make no mistake. This is a business with great ambition.

"You know," Steve confides, when the Craggy Range vineyards in the Gimblett Gravels in Hawkes Bay are reached, "I noticed that Calvin Klein logo, that distinctive KC, on the back of someone's jeans and on a tee-shirt and I thought, "that's what I want" and that was the brief I gave the designer." If you look closely, then, at the Craggy Range label you will see a smart C and a cute R. If you look closely at the wines? Then you will see so much more.

Art Deco grapes in Napier

In 1931 the old town of Napier was flattened by an earthquake registering nearly eight on the Richter scale. The town was rebuilt and much of that rebuilding followed the prevailing architectural and design precepts of the time. Napier is today celebrated as "the world's Art Deco township". The abundance of appropriate architecture, though modest and provincial, some false, some Spanish mission style, with a little sprinkling of Art Nouveau, is striking. The most famous putative Art Deco building in town, the National Tobacco Company building, is indeed more Art Nouveau than Art Deco. The entrance's false *vaussoirs*, created by extended rose stems from the archivolt, are most decidedly Art Deco, but the door furniture seems to sit, charmingly it must be said, between the two. Art Deco is about shadow and line, diminishment of grandeur, and form following function and this is most evident in the compact exteriors of the domestic houses rather than the commercial structures.

At the C J Pask winery there is no Art Deco evident, but there are some elegant whites and reds. The most impressive, amongst a Sauvignon Blanc, a Gimblett Road Chardonnay, a Hawkes Bay Reserve Chardonnay, a Gimblett Road Pinot Noir, a Gimblett Road Merlot, a C J Pask Reserve Merlot, and a Hawkes Bay Declaration Cabernet Sauvignon/Malbec/Merlot, is the Gimblett Road Cabernet/Merlot. It has coffee and cocoa fruit and a lush tannin structure which gives it some serious heft and weight. Kate Radburnd, the winemaker here (and managing director and co-partner), exudes the air of someone uncommonly committed and bold. I also liked some structural effects of the Pinot, with its dry savouriness. Her colleague, Bill Nancarrow, says that growing it was a lot easier than when he attempted to make Pinot in Leatherhead (which is like asking a surfer to try his luck in the Thames estuary).

"You made Pinot Noir in England? In Surrey?" I gasp. "Nope. The grapes didn't go through *veraison*." In other words, the grapes simply couldn't ripen.

Big but delicate

Montana may be the biggest Kiwi wine company by a huge margin and it may account for a massive seventy per cent of Kiwi wines sold, but there is no doubt that the ones it makes at Church Road in Hawkes Bay, and markets under that label, are individual, recognizably hand-crafted, and remarkably well-focussed as expressions of their grape varieties. Winemaker Tony Pritchard has a delicate touch.

The Sauvignon Blanc has classic mineralized complexity. "Nice noise in the background," says Tony mysteriously. "Something happening, you know?" he adds helpfully.

The wine is "more Pessac-Léognan than Loire", he adds further. He means it has the crunchy richness which great white Graves achieve rather than the lean grassiness of Loire Sauvignons. It's a blend of sixty per cent Hawkes Bay juice and forty per cent Marlborough.

The Hawkes Bay Chardonnay, the top selling Chardonnay in Kiwi restaurants, is elegant and cool. The Hawkes Bay Reserve Chardonnay from the Korokiko vineyard has superb oak and fruit integration and a lovely buttery-textured finish of gentle smokiness.

The Cuvée Series Chardonnay has great length of flavour rounding off a toasted seed bouquet. It's a wine to decant at least five to seven hours before serving. The Virtu Noble Semillon has a rich Barsac-like aroma (crème brûlée and wax) and it is remarkable (well, at NZ$40/£15 the half bottle it ought to be).

On the red side, the Cabernet Sauvignon/Merlot/Cab Franc/Malbec has impact yet elegance, finesse yet power. The tannins are classy. The Reserve Merlot/Cabernet parades cassis, plums, and though fresh and full of developmental potential has the sort of tannins I want in my blood stream today. It's an invigorating wine.

Sacred Hill

David Mason, Sacred Hill's managing director, has built a superb restaurant and visitor's facility and created a must-visit winery – just as winemaker Tony Bish has created must-taste wines.

Tony discusses his winemaking philosophy: "Hands-off winemaking I call it," he says. "We've spent five years monitoring wild yeast. We don't use enzymes. No sulphur before bottling."

I thought the Marlborough Sauvignon Blanc was a complete wine (and completely scrumptious). The Hawkes Bay Barrel-Fermented Sauvignon Blanc was succulent. The Sauvage Sauvignon Blanc was stunningly textured and sinuously complex. The Whitecliff Vineyards Chardonnay had lovely oily, peachy fruit. The Hawkes Bay Barrel-Fermented Chardonnay, with its pineapple and smoky pear, was impressively tailored. The Rifleman's Chardonnay was powerful, like a richer style of Montrachet. The Cairnbrae Clansman Chardonnay had tamed its US oak influence to be elegant on the finish. The Cairnbrae Pinot Gris was dry and peachy. The Cairnbrae Old River Riesling was tangy and dry to finish.

On Sacred Hill's red side I enjoyed the immensely quaffable Whitecliff Vineyards Merlot. I warmed to the Basket Press Merlot/Cabernet 2000 with its plump fruit. I adored the Helmsman Cabernet Sauvignon with its stunning tannins, and I gagged with delight over the Brokenstone Merlot with its coffee beans, nuts, tannins, liquorice, and surging finish.

Science versus Intuition

Esk Valley winery is owned by Villa Maria, New Zealand's second biggest winery group, and Gordon Russell is the winemaker. Darryl Brooker, assistant winemaker (who started his working life as a naval gunner), was deputed to show me the ropes and makes out a cogent case for working for a big company in a subsidiary winery.

"We concentrate on high quality here. But without the large company behind us we couldn't do that. We get to operate as a small concern, not the branch of a big one which is told what to think." Darryl is fervent in his admiration of Gordon Russell and his approach.

"I worked at Mount Adam in Oz before. It was the scientific approach there. At Esk there is emphasis on feel and taste. Let the wine make itself. Let's not let chemistry have too much say. I've learned a lot from Gordon."

The wines have charm. The Black Label Riesling shows dry honey and lime sherbet; the Sauvignon Blanc tangy acids. The Chenin Blanc is excellent structurally with a waxy honey undertone. The Pinot Gris is a touch too alcoholic but has some nutty/apricotty elegance. The NZ$15 (£5.70) Chardonnay is terrific lip smackin' stuff with low acids and a creamy richness. A Chardonnay is a touch barrel-raw on the finish, but it has some amusing woodiness. The Black Label Merlot/Cabernet Sauvignon is fantastic value at less than twenty bucks, for it offers leather, polished fruit, and finely integrated tannins. The Reserve Merlot/Cabernet Sauvignon has Hell's Angels tannins yet to soften (as Hell's Angels always do with time), but cellar it eighteen months from vintage release and a really extruded wine of concentration and class will emerge.

Licence to innovate

Vidal Estate, another Villa Maria subsidiary, is famous as being the first winery in New Zealand to take advantage of changes in local licensing laws to open a bar and restaurant in 1979. Winemaker Rod MacDonald makes a range of intriguing wines: Syrah; Merlot; Malbec; Pinot Noir; Viognier; Chardonnay; and Cabernet Franc. These wines were all extremely tightly focussed and well-made, but the three which stood out were the Gimblett Gravels Cabernet Sauvignon, the Reserve Merlot/Cabernet, and the Newton Forrest Vineyard Pinot Noir.

Gisborne

Beauty spot

Annie and James Millton are a beautiful couple. The phrase "beautiful couple" is more commonly found amongst gossip column trivia but the Milltons are opening bats for New Zealand in the middle-aged category because they are not only untouched and handsome, but beautifully at peace with one another, though their world is a struggle. This is the struggle, each year, to produce wine by Biodynamic methods. Millton Vineyard is Gisborne's most remarkable wine producer.

James is sympathetic to my theory on UV light in NZ: "What you're suggesting about phenols and UV is right on the nail. At Millton we leaf pluck the inside leaves and leave the outside leaves as an umbrella. It's considered a risk, but when I worked a vintage in Burgundy we rejected any grapes with sun-burn on them and many Kiwi grapes are picked sunburnt."

However, on other matters, germane to the theme of this book, he does not see eye to eye with me: "I am the first New World wine-grower (not winemaker you note and I make a distinction) to be asked back to the Old World to teach – or rather I'd like to say teach but let's say discuss – to discuss the ancient techniques of Biodynamism. They want me to come back and show them the old ways which many of them have forgotten. This is Biodynamics."

He has strong views on this subject: "Everybody in New Zealand," he says, smiling with the smile of someone about to touch on the subject of a beloved best friend's risible eccentricity or hellish halitosis, "is so anal about Pinot Noir. We have conferences on it and discuss it, but there's nothing said about Biodynamics. And Biodynamism is a growing trend in Burgundy. There's Comte de Lafon, Lalou Bize-Leroy, Leflaive..."

Auckland...

Beginning with Cooper's Creek

The Marlborough Sauvignon Blanc here is perfectly balanced with a lovely bright lilt of fruit on the finish. The Marlborough Reserve Sauvignon Blanc is tighter and has more finely extruded fruit than the basic version. The Unoaked Gisborne Chardonnay has a light sprinkling of lemon on its finish. The Hawkes Bay Chardonnay shows a wonderful oily richness of lemon, gooseberry, and melon tinged with a gentle creamy smokiness.

The Marlborough Riesling is lightly tangy and understated, elegant, subtle stuff. The Marlborough Pinot Noir has a certain elegance. The Hawkes Bay Merlot possesses soft tannins and is well balanced. The Gardener Merlot/Cabernet Sauvignon has soft tannins and a light touch of vegetal pepper. The Viognier is world-class.

Overall these are commercial in the least commercial way, with smooth delivery of fruit and a highly drinkable immediacy of balanced richness.

Dalmatian, no spots.

Michael Brajkovich's forebearers came from Dalmatia. His vineyards lie in West Auckland at Kumeu River. He uses only natural yeasts (though with a stuck ferment he inoculates, which purists insist destroys the integrity of any natural yeasts since the vineyard and winery will develop a strain based on the commercial one).

Brajkovich Kumeu Chardonnay is clean yet rich. Kumeu River Chardonnay (an alarming 14% ABV) is tangy and ripe. Kumeu River Mate's Vineyard Chardonnay is very citrousy. Kumeu River Pinot Gris is also distinctly tangy and acidically challenging. An older Chardonnay has an interesting orange peel undertone, but again that tangy trademark. On the red side the Pinot Noir is vegetal, a little raw. The Kumeu River Melba Merlot/Malbec shows some alcohol on the finish. It's a distinctly unKiwi style, more northern European. It's a story of the winemaker calling all the shots all the way.

Villa Maria: sitting on a volcano

Villa Maria's new winery complex in Mangere, Auckland, is set within the crater of an extinct volcano called Ihumatao. It last blew its top, according to local volcanologists, 20,000 years ago. It looks peaceful and bucolic now.

One of the great strengths – indeed, the greatest strength – of the NZ wine industry is that its two major players, Montana and Villa Maria, can produce such excellent wines. VM has shown itself to be innovative and fleet-of-foot. It was the first major player to move to screwcaps. It is, perhaps, only conservative in its labelling categorization which has Reserve at the top, Cellar Selection in the middle, and Private Bin at the bottom. Dull words. Very far from dull wines.

Tasting seventeen wines in Ihumatao's crater, which has topsoil deep enough and wide enough to accommodate a vineyard as well as a production facility and offices, is an experience. The earth doesn't move, but the palate is exercised.

Private Bin Sauvignon Blanc is finely concentrated and one of NZ's best expressions of this grape. Cellar Selection Sauvignon Blanc is classier, and has a touch of rich grass. Reserve Wairau Valley Sauvignon Blanc has sleek peach on the finish. Reserve Clifford Bay Sauvignon Blanc is stuffed with lemon and has a herbaceous undertone. Private Bin East Coast Chardonnay has creamy gentility. Cellar Selection Marlborough Chardonnay shows a gentle burnt aroma and rich, vegetal, lightly woody fruit. Reserve Marlborough Chardonnay is deliciously toasty and nutty. Private Bin Riesling has a beautiful texture and good plump fruit. Cellar Selection Riesling is concentrated, finely balanced. Reserve Riesling is towards the off-dry, has tangy fruit, and is perfect for Thai food.

On to the reds: Cellar Selection Pinot Noir is, bouquet aside (a little unfocussed here), one of the driest and classiest on the finish. It has superb mid-palate black cherry fruit and positive tannins. Lloyd Single Vineyard Pinot Noir has more evolved tannins, but, oddly, juicier fruit and is thus less gripping on the finish. Reserve Pinot Noir is savoury and rich with a touch of tobacco. Cellar Selection Merlot/Cabernet is couth, polished, mature, and has superb tannins. Reserve Merlot/Cabernet is chunkier than the last wine and the tannins are fresher. Reserve Merlot/Cabernet is hugely quaffable with its superbly soft tannins and fruit/acid balance of a high, handsomely developed order. Reserve Merlot Hawkes Bay is superlative with magnificent chewy fruit, chocolate and cassis and leather fruit, a hint of raspberry and meaty tannins. It is one of the most convincing Merlots made in New Zealand.

The quiet driving force behind Villa Maria is proprietor and managing director George Fistonich. He is a benign and dynamic employer who has steered Villa Maria into the position of having the most cohesive image of any NZ wine producer. Montana may be bigger, but its range is a curate's egg. Cloudy Bay has more prestige, because of one single wine, its Sauvignon Blanc. But no other large NZ wine company has such a solid reliable reputation as VM, whatever the vintage, whatever the price of the wine, whatever the variety. Its marketing appears exemplary, its labelling consistent and classy (and not liable to whackiness or constant fiddling). A VM wine is an affordable luxury.

Microcosmic Waiheke Island
Wee, a bit twee

This is the most romantic wine region in New Zealand. Fittingly, it is left to last because it wholly justifies my belief that it is people who make wine not vineyards. Of the island's handful of producers, each and every one is dramatically represented by his/her wines – in personality, ego, ambition, and outlook.

Obsidian's Chester Nichols, on just nine hectares of vines, produces 1,500 cases of wine from Cabernet Sauvignon, Merlot, Cabernet Franc, and Malbec grapes. "It's ego with me," he says. "I want to make the best Cabernet/Merlot in New Zealand. I'm an extremist. I have nothing else to live for. Winemakers have celebrity status here. I want to be on TV and talk about my wine." Since revealing this ambition, he has left to become a photographer.

At Stonyridge – a fashion boutique which makes wine and sells food (it also grows olives) – one encounters a brand with a well-managed set of values. Stephen White is the owner. His top wine is Larose. It is the most expensive wine in New Zealand, averaging NZ$98 (£37) at auction. I tasted the 2000 of this Cabernet Sauvignon, Merlot, Malbec, Cabernet Franc, Petit Verdot blend and was no more thrilled by it than if it had been a NZ$15 (£5.70) Spanish Garnacha. That's my crude palate for you.

Geoff Creighton owns Peninsula Estate, just six hectares of vines, but his main commercial activity – since six hectares is hardly a self-supporting amount of sod – is Leigh Lobster, which exports crayfish to Asia and the US. The wines are highly extracted; their focus seems elsewhere.

At Mudbrick, proprietor Nick Jones produces a Reserve Syrah that is rich and warm, but a touch hot on the finish, and a Shepherd's Point Cabernet Sauvignon/Merlot 2000, which is his best wine with its savoury tannins, also showing heat on the finish. Mudbrick has chaptalized its wines.

Waiheke Vineyard is a family affair run by the Dunleavys, father Terry and sons John and Paul. They produce wines under the Te Motu label. They've been at it since 1988, though the first grape crush wasn't until 1993. The wines have a cosy feel, but the focus is good. They are relaxed, not trying too hard to flatter. They are bottled at Matua, over at Kumeu in Greater Auckland.

Tony Forsyth of Te Whau (pronounced Tee-F-ow) owns both an impressive vineyard and a striking restaurant. Tony, a psychologist by training – who became a "human resources consultant" before the rat race, and its particular breed of flea-prone rats, exhausted his patience – produced his first wines here in 1999. If Waiheke is an insular convocation of male egos all trying to make great red wine, then Tony is the urbane master of them all. He understands people, brands, product appeal, trends, and he has a firm grasp of natural charm (he was born with it, by the bucket load). He wants to go organic for his vines and he wants those vines, he says, to make one of the best reds in the world. His

measure is not just other Waiheke reds, or other New Zealand reds; his measure is what the world considers, for good or ill, great red wine. Te Whau's The Point, a Cabernets Sauvignon and Franc/Merlot/Malbec blend, is a promising start.

At Miro there is man and wife Barnett Bond and Catherine Vosper. "I do lots of other stuff other than make wine. I write a wine column for a medical journal. I advise the government on certain medical matters," Barnett reveals. Catherine and he have just two hectares of wines, but acres and acres of heart. I tasted a Bordeaux blend, lacking in mid-palate character. This slim, elegant couple do not yet make slim, elegant wines. They will certainly do so, in time.

The wines to which everyone on Waiheke must bend the knee bear the name Goldwater. When the Goldwaters first sailed here in their yacht in the 1970s, it was a backwater. In those days buying property on the island was cheap. Now you can attend in-house Sunday auction sales where the auctioneer takes bids for the property from an assembled crowd as well as by phone from people in Wellington or even London. Property prices nowadays are exorbitant. NZ$600,000 (£227,200) was the figure reached when the bidding stopped at the last auction I attended for an ugly clapboard dwelling of no architectural sensitivity and with an abandoned motorhome in the driveway.

Kim and Jeanette Goldwater put Waiheke on the map. They started with a hectare of Cabernet Sauvignon in 1978. "All we really wanted to do was make a bit of red wine for ourselves and our friends," Kim has said. 1982 was the first vintage, released for sale in 1985, and since then the the estate has grown in size (it now has fourteen hectares on Waiheke and makes wine from vineyards elsewhere), reputation, and kudos. The local council should give Kim and Jeanette Goldwater the freedom of the island. Once just a hippy hangout, half an hour from Auckland harbour across the bay by ferry, it's now got a designer feel.

So have wine prices. In Spring 2005, a bottle of Goldwater New Dog Marlborough Sauvignon Blanc 2003 was knocked down at the Houston Rodeo International Wine Competition and Auction in Texas for US$13,500 (£7,740). Admittedly, it was a six-litre bottle (equivalent to eight bottles and called a Methuselah) and it had won a gold medal in the Houston Rodeo competition. It's probably the highest price ever paid for a bottle of Kiwi wine. And it was a suitable commemoration of twenty years of Goldwater vintages.

Having dinner at the estate, Kim once produced a ten-year-old Cabernet/Merlot from his cellar which flew superbly in the face of all my theories about New Zealand wines not ageing with dignity. It was a perfectly textured, aromatic, sensual mouthful of fruit. Anyone who tasted it would conclude that its region of production was indeed world class; however, since we have to add Kim and Jeanette into this terroir equation to make sense, a rational being would also conclude that it is necessary to clone the Goldwaters.

LEFT You read about the influence of Jurassic soils on vineyards, but in Sam Neill's case (shown here with wife Toriko holding their bottled pride and joy) it is more *Jurassic Park*. Sam's successful movie career means he is amply able to underwrite his Two Paddocks vineyard in its picturesque Central Otago setting. Sam has a Mephistophelian expression which is changed by a subtle smile. He can play a villain or a hero or, as with *The Dish*, that brilliant Aussie movie of 2001, be an avuncular pipe smoking star-gazer. In Otago he has more settled roles: husband, father (to the gorgeous Elena), neighbour, and enthusiastic Pinot Noir producer. Without doubt, his personality infuses the wine.

RIGHT-HAND PAGE

TOP If you get bored with looking at vines, New Zealand has many other scenic options.

BELOW LEFT Kim and Jeannette Goldwater were the first to produce wines on Waiheke Island and theirs are still the most consistently honest.

BELOW RIGHT Te Mata Estate, Hawkes Bay, is NZ's oldest, dating from 1890. Owner John Buck is a former chairman of the New Zealand Wine Institute, the benevolent bureaucracy which does so much to promote Kiwi wines overseas.

LEFT-HAND PAGE

TOP Kai Schubert (right) and partner Marion Deimling at Martinborough's Aylestone Lodge enjoying their unique Tribianco white wine (a blend of Chardonnay, Pinot Gris, and Muller-Thurgau). Pinot Noir is Kai's obsession, however, and he will surely soon produce one of the area's finest.

CENTRE LEFT Stainless steel is at the heart of the NZ wine industry's success. The technology has existed in the extensive local dairy industry for years and so it was easy for wineries to find the equipment and the engineers to install it.

CENTRE RIGHT Marlborough is famous for Sauvignon Blanc, but Grove Mill's winemaker, Dave Pearce, also turns out a feisty Merlot (he's a dab hand with a trout rod, too).

BOTTOM A yard sale of second-hand stainless-steel equipment will not go short of customers.

RIGHT-HAND PAGE

TOP Auckland is bustling yet never brash, modern but not all surface, bright without being dazzling.

BOTTOM LEFT You can find secret places in New Zealand to swim undisturbed. This is mine.

BOTTOM RIGHT They said anyone who tries to grow grapes on Waiheke Island was bananas. Now the Island has twenty-four wineries (and a few banana trees).

New Zealand's winemaker

SOUTH ISLAND

CENTRAL OTAGO

AKARUA
Cairnmuir Rd, Bannockburn (POBox 120, Cromwell).Tel: 3 445 3211
warren@akarua.com. www.akarua.com
Winemaker: Carol Bunn

ALEXANDRA WINE CO
75 Rockview Rd, Alexandra
Tel: 3 448 8872. Fax: 3 448 8537
alexwine@es.co.nz
Winemaker: Carol Bunn

BLACK RIDGE VINEYARD & WINERY
Conroy's Rd, RD 1, (PO Box 54)
Alexandra.Tel: 3 449 2059
blackridge@clear.net.nz
www.blackridge.co.nz
Winemaker: Kevin Clark

CARRICK
Bannockburn, RD2, Cromwell, New Zealand.Tel: 3 445 3480. Fax 3 445 3481
wines@carrick.co.nz. www.carrick.co.nz
Winemaker: Steve Davies

CHARD FARM
Chard Rd, SH 6, Gibbston, RD 1, Queenstown
Tel: 3 442 6110. Fax: 3 441 8400
sales@chardfarm.co.nz
www.chardfarm.co.nz
Winemaker: John Wallace

DRY GULLY
Earnscleugh Road, RD 1, Alexandra
Tel: 3 449 2930
Winemaker: Dean Shaw

FELTON RD
RD 2, Bannockburn
Tel: 3 445 0885. Fax: 3 445 0881
wines@feltonroad.com
www.feltonroad.com
Winemaker: Blair Walter

GIBBSTON VALLEY WINES
SH 6, Gibbston, RD 1, Queenstown
Tel: 3 442 6910. Fax: 3 442 6909
info@gvwines.co.nz. www.gvwines.co.nz
Winemaker: Grant Taylor

MOUNT DIFFICULTY WINES
Felton Rd, Bannockburn, (PO Box 69, Cromwell).Tel: 3 443 8398
info@mtdifficulty.co.nz
www.mtdifficulty.co.nz
Winemaker: Matt Dicey

OLSSENS GARDEN VINEYARD
306 Felton Rd, Bannockburn, RD 2, Cromwell.Tel: 3 445 1716. Fax: 3 445 0050
wine@olssens.co.nz. www.olssens.co.nz
Winemaker: Peter Bartle

QUARTZ REEF
Building 6, Lake Dunstan Estate, McNulty Rd, (PO Box 63) Cromwell
Tel: 3 445 3084. Fax: 3 445 3086
info@quartzreef.co.nz
www.quartzreef.co.nz
Winemakers: Rudi Bauer, Andreas Bassier

RIPPON VINEYARD & WINERY
246 Mt Aspiring Rd, (PO Box 175), Lake Wanaka 9192
Tel: 3 443 8084. Fax: 3 443 8034
lois.mills@rippon.co.nz
www.rippon.co.nz
Winemaker: Nick Mills

TWO PADDOCKS
PO Box 369, Queenstown
Tel: 3 449 2756. Fax: 3 449 2755
webmaster@twopaddocks.com
www.twopaddocks.com
Winemaker: Dean Shaw

WAIPARA

OMIHI HILLS
92 Reeces Rd, RD 3, Amberley 8251
Tel: 3 314 5901
www.danielschusterwines.com
Winemaker: Daniel Schuster

PEGASUS BAY
Stockgrove Road, RD 2, Amberley, Waipara, North Canterbury
Tel: 3 314 6869. Fax: 3 314 6861
info@pegasusbay.com
www.pegasusbay.com
Winemaker: Matthew Donaldson

NELSON

NEUDORF ESTATE
Neudorf RD, RD 2, Upper Moutere, Nelson.Tel: 3 543 2643
wine@neudorf.co.nz. www.neudorf.co.nz
Winemakers: Tim Finn, John Kavanagh

SEIFRIED ESTATE
Redwood Rd, Appleby, (POBox 7020), Nelson.Tel: 3 544 5599. Fax: 3 544 5522
wines@seifried.co.nz. www.seifried.co.nz
Winemaker: Christopher Seifried

NORTH ISLAND

MARLBOROUGH
ALLAN SCOTT
Jacksons Road, RD 3, Blenheim,
Marlborough
Tel: 3 572 9054. Fax: 3 572 9053
info@allanscott.com
www.allanscott.com
Winemaker: Josh Scott

CLOUDY BAY
PO Box 376, Blenheim, Marlborough
Tel: 3 520 9140. Fax: 3 520 9040
info@cloudybay.co.nz. www.cloudybay.co.nz
Winemaker: Kevin Judd

GROVE MILL WINERY
Cnr SH 63 & Waihopai Valley Rd,
(PO Box 67), Renwick, Malborough
Tel: 3 572 8200. Fax: 3 572 8211
info@grovemill.co.nz. www.grovemill.co.nz
Winemakers: David Pearce, SarahInkersell

HERZOG
81 Jeffries Rd, RD3, Blenheim
Tel: 3 572 8770
info@herzog.co.uk
www.herzog.co.nz
Winemaker: Hans Herzog

HIGHFIELD ESTATE
Brookby Rd, RD 2, Blenheim
Tel: 3 572 9244. Fax: 3 572 9257
winery@highfield.co.nz
www.highfield.co.nz
Winemaker: Alistair Soper

HUIA VINEYARDS
Boyces Rd, RD 3, (PO Box 92, Renwick),
Malborough. Tel: 3 572 8326. Fax: 3 572 8331
wine@huia.net.nz. www.huia.net.nz
Winemakers: Mike & Claire Allan

ISABEL ESTATE VINEYARD
72 Hawkesbury Rd, (PO Box 29), Renwick,
Marlborough
Tel: 3 572 8300. Fax: 3 572 8383
info@isabelestate.com
www.isabelestate.com
Winemaker: Anthony Moore

JACKSON ESTATE
107 Jacksons Rd, (PO Box 102, Renwick),
Blenheim. Tel: 3 572 8287
jacksonestate@xtra.co.nz
www.jacksonestate.co.nz
Winemakers: Martin Shaw, Michael
Paterson

JOHANNESHOF CELLARS
SH 1, Koromiko, RD 3, Blenheim
Tel: 3 573 7035. Fax: 3 573 7034
johanneshof.cellars@xtra.co.nz
www.johanneshof.co.nz
Winemakers: Warwick Foley, Edel Everling

LAWSON'S DRY HILLS WINES
238 Alabama Rd, (PO Box 4020) Blenheim
Tel: 3 578 7674. Fax: 3 578 7603
wine@lawsonsdryhills.co.nz
www.lawsonsdryhills.co.nz
Winemakers: Mike Just, Marcus Wright

**MONTANA BRANCOTT WINERY
VISITOR CENTRE**
Main Rd South, SH 1, Riverlands,
Marlborough, (PO Box 331) Blenheim
Tel: 3 577 5777
brancottcellardoor@montanawines.co.nz
www.montanawines.co.nz
Winemaker: Patrick Materman

NAUTILUS ESTATE
12 Rapaura Rd, (PO Box 107, Renwick),
Blenheim. Tel: 3 572 9364. Fax: 3 572 9374
sales@nautilusestate.com
www.nautilusestate.com
Winemaker: Clive Jones

SERESIN ESTATE
Bedford Rd, (PO Box 859) Blenheim
Tel: 3 572 9408. Fax: 3 572 9850
kate@seresin.co.nz
www.seresin.co.nz
Winemaker: Brian Bicknell

WITHER HILLS VINEYARD
211 New Renwick RD, RD 2, Blenheim
(89A Seaview Rd, Remuera, Auckland)
Tel: 9 522 9684. Fax: 9 522 9685
winery@witherhills.co.nz
www.witherhills.co.nz
Winemakers: Brent Marris, Ben Glover

MARTINBOROUGH
DRY RIVER WINES
Puruatanga Rd, (PO Box 72),
Martinborough
Tel: 6 306 9388. Fax: 6 306 9275
info@dryriver.co.nz. www.dryriver.co.nz
Winemaker: Neil McCallum

MARTINBOROUGH VINEYARD
Princess St, (PO Box 85), Martinborough
Tel: 6 306 9955. Fax: 6 306 9217
winery@mvwine.co.nz
www.martinborough-vineyard.co.nz
Winemaker: Claire Mulholland

**PALLISER ESTATE WINES OF
MARTINBOROUGH**
Kitchener St, (PO Box 121) Martinborough
Tel: 6 306 9019. palliser@palliser.co.nz
www.palliser.co.nz
Winemaker: Allan Johnson

TE KAIRANGA WINES
Martins Rd (POBox 52) Martinborough
Tel: 6 306 9122. Fax: 6 306 9322
info@tekairanga.co.nz
www.tkwine.co.nz
Winemaker: Peter Caldwell

HAWKES BAY
CJ PASK WINERY
1133 Omahu Rd, (PO Box 849) Hastings
Tel: 6 879 7906. Fax: 6 879 6428
info@cjpaskwinery.co.nz
www.cjpaskwinery.co.nz
Winemakers: Kate Radburnd,
Russell Wiggins

CRAGGY RANGE VINEYARDS
253 Waimarama Rd, (PO Box 8749),
Havelock North
Tel: 6 873 7126. Fax: 6 873 7141
info@craggyrange.com
www.craggyrange.com
Winemaker: Doug Wisor

ESK VALLEY ESTATE
Main Rd, (PO Box 111) Bay View, Napier
Tel: 6 836 6411. Fax: 6 836 6413
enquiries@eskvalley.co.nz
www.eskvalley.co.nz
Winemaker: Gordon Russell

SACRED HILL
Cellar door: 1033 Dartmoor Rd, Puketapu,
Napier. Admin: 1472 Omahu Rd, (James
Rochford Place, RD 5), Hastings
Tel: 6 879 8760. www.sacredhill.com
enquiries@sacredhill.com
Winemaker: Tony Bish

VIDAL ESTATE
913 St Aubyn St East, (PO Box 48)
Hastings. Tel: 6 876 5891
enquiries@vidalestate.co.nz
www.vidal.co.nz
Winemaker: Rod McDonald

WEST AUCKLAND
COOPERS CREEK VINEYARDS
601 SH 16, Huapai (PO Box 140, Kumeu)
Tel: 9 412 8560. Fax: 9 412 8375
info@cooperscreek.co.nz
www.cooperscreek.co.nz
Winemaker: Simon Nunns

KUMEU RIVER WINES
550 SH 16, (PO Box 24) Kumeu
Tel: 9 412 8415. Fax: 9 412 7627
enquiries@kumeuriver.co.nz
www.kumeuriver.co.nz
Winemaker: Michael Brajkovich MW

VILLA MARIA
Paynters/New Renwick Road, Fairhall,
Blenheim, Marlborough
Tel: 3 577 9530. Fax: 3 577 9585
enquiries@villamaria.co.nz
www.villamaria.co.nz
Winemaker: Alastair Maling MW

SOUTH AND CENTRAL AUCKLAND
MONTANA WINES
171 Pilkington Rd, Glen Innes,
(PO Box 18-293) Auckland
Tel: 9 570 8400. Fax: 9 372 6827
information@montanawines.co.nz
www.montanawines.co.nz
Winemakers: Jeff Clarke, Jane Dewitt,
Alex Kahl

WAIHEKE ISLAND
GOLDWATER ESTATE
18 Causeway Rd, Putiki Bay, Waiheke
Island. Tel: 9 372 7493. Fax: 9 372 6827
info@goldwaterwine.co.nz
www.goldwaterwine.com
Winemakers: Kim Goldwater, Nikolai
St George

MIRO VINEYARD
Browns Rd, Onetangi, Waiheke Island
Tel: 9 372 7854. miro@xtra.co.nz
www.winefind.co.nz
Winemaker: Barnett Bond

MUDBRICK VINEYARD
Church Bay Rd, (PO Box 130) Oneroa,
Waiheke Island. Tel: 9 372 9050
Fax: 9 372 9051. mudbrick@ihug.co.nz
www.mudbrick.co.nz
Winemaker: James Rowan

OBSIDIAN VINEYARD
Te Makiri Rd, (PO Box 345) Waiheke
Island. Tel: 9 372 6100
info@obsidian.co.nz
www.waihekewine.co.nz
Winemaker: Simon Nunns

PENINSULA ESTATE WINES
52A Korora Rd, Oneroa, Waiheke Island
Tel: 9 372 7866. Fax: 9 372 7840
wines@peninsulaestate.co.nz
www.peninsulaestate.com
Winemaker: Christopher Lush

STONYRIDGE VINEYARD

80 Onetangi Rd, (PO Box 265, Ostend),
Waiheke Island
Tel: 9 372 8822. Fax: 9 372 8766
info@stonyridge.co.nz
www.stonyridge.co.nz
Winemaker: Martin Mackenzie

TE MOTU

76 Onetangi Rd (PO Box 33114), Waiheke
Tel: 9 486 3859. Fax: 9 486 2341
terry@winezeal.co.nz
www.temotu.co.nz
Winemaker: Michael Brajkovich

TE WHAU VINEYARD

218 Te Whau Dr, (PO Box 167, Oneroa)
Waiheke Island
Tel: 9 372 7191. Fax: 9 372 7189
tony@tewhau.com
www.tewhau.com
Winemaker: Herb Friedli

GISBORNE
THE MILLTON VINEYARD

Papatu Road, (PO Box 66) Manutuke,
Gisborne
Tel: 6 862 8680. Fax: 6 862 8869
info@millton.co.nz. www.millton.co.nz
Winemaker: James Milton

MONTANA GISBORNE WINERY

Lytton Rd, (POBox 1374) Gisborne
Tel: 6 867 9819
information@montanawines.co.nz
www.montanawines.co.nz
Winemakers: Steve Voysey, Brent Laidlaw

South Africa

CAPE OF GREAT BIG HOPES.

"So the miracle came after all."
Alan Paton, *Too Late The Phalarope* (1953).

RIGHT Arniston Bay – in the waters of which Right Whales disport – has given its name to a very successful Cape wine brand. It's almost as far south as you can get in Africa, though Cape Agulhas, a little further along and down, claims that distinction.

The incredible confidence and chutzpah that the Cape region can now muster is a reflection of how far South Africa as a unified nation has come in so short a time. In a dozen years from the time Nelson Mandela was released, it has acquired a spring in its step and a confident attitude. One can almost feel sympathy for the old established wine exporters of Europe. Battling against the dynamic Australasians, Californians, and the dashing South Americans is tough enough, but now there is this other beast, one of a most exotic, attractive, and virile demeanour. The Cape produces around 650 million litres of wine; in the world league table it is number eight, turning out three per cent of the world's wine and exporting to over 100 countries.

The vineyards, over 300 years old now, are confined to the Cape. There are some 110,000 hectares of these, grown under sixty official geographical designations (or appellations). As taxonomically tedious as California, the Cape delights in organizing itself in a determined bureaucratic fashion into regions, districts, and wards (the smallest). A ward can get itself upgraded to a district (Walker Bay for example) yet a district may not be part of a region (Walker Bay again). A ward can be out by itself and not subsumed within a region (Elim). Not very exciting? We will content ourselves here with looking at Constantia, Franschhoek, Stellenbosch, Durbanville, Elim, Olifants River, Paarl, Robertson, Swartland, Tulbagh, Somerset West/Walker Bay, and Worcester. The major grape varieties are Chenin Blanc (sometimes called Steen), Chardonnay, Colombard, Muscat, Riesling, and Sauvignon Blanc, amongst the whites (a little Semillon and Viognier are planted also). The reds are Pinotage, Cabernet Sauvignon, Merlot, Cinsault (spelt Cinsaut), Ruby Cabernet, Pinot Noir, and Shiraz (there are also minor plantings of some Italian and Portuguese varieties, as well as Cabernet Franc, Malbec, and Mourvedre). Any exported wine must be eighty-five per cent of a single variety to qualify for that status.

Stellenbosch
Style, substance, finesse… and huge confidence

Ken and Theresa Forrester live just outside Stellenbosch. They keep vines, dogs, horses, and geese. "The geese love vineyard snails," says Theresa. "Their gorges get so swollen with eating them the birds become lopsided and topple over."

Theresa has a Meissen china quality to her arrangement of limbs. Theresa and Ken are well paired. Ken's white hair sets him off perfectly against Theresa's elegance like milk in a jug.

A tasting of Forrester wines offers a similar coherence yet contrasting set of styles. One of the most impressive is the Forrester Family Reserve Sauvignon Blanc which offers satsuma peel, green pepper, and melon – and peach. More startling is a Noble Late Harvest Botrytized Chenin Blanc, the honeyed richness and fine acidity of which will see the wine through the next thirty years. As if this were insufficient climax to the tasting – conducted in the living room (furnished with the same relaxed finesse exhibited by the family and its wines) – then Ken Forrester's remark as this deliriously sweet wine is swished around the palate is utterly deliciously Mosaic. "Try it with sushi," he proclaims. "It's like a message from God."

Dinner at 96 Winery Road, Ken's own restaurant (off the R44 between Somerset West and Stellenbosch), proves that messages from God are highly edible. It's chef Natasha Harris's day off, so God's messenger slices the sashimi himself; prepares green mustard, soy sauce, and pickled ginger. Sashimi and sushi go wonderfully with sweet Chenin Blanc.

The Jordans

It was Gary Jordan's dad who bought the vineyard originally, as a place to build a house and get away from the family shoe business (the Jordan great-grandfather came from Groby, a suburb of Leicester, a city that was once the footwear-making capital of the UK and Empire). So Gary has been around to see a lot of changes in the Cape in ten years. "The winemakers," Gary says, "are far more closely involved in growing grapes than they used to be."

There is no doubt, to the mind of this observer, that the quality of the grapes coming off the vines has increased dramatically too. With the improvements come harvesting machines of which the Jordans are newly in possession. This, according to Kathy Jordan, permits picking at night when "it is inhuman to expect pickers to work". I would have thought that for a few weeks a year people would be happy to earn extra for night work and to pick grapes away from the heat of the sun. In a land of vast untapped labour resources, much of it hanging around street corners hoping for work, machines could be said to be a luxury. But then the Jordans do produce a most luxurious, puckishly tannic top-of-the-range Cabernet Sauvignon.

TOP LEFT Simon Barlow of Rustenberg has a farm to run as well as a winery business.

TOP RIGHT Giorgio della Cia's wines at Meerlust live up unashamedly, robustly, welcomingly, to their old-fashioned labelling.

BELOW Rustenberg is hardly alone amongst Cape wine estates in providing dramatic scenery wherever you care to look: here, the Simonsberg looms large.

Beyerskloof

Beyers Truter looks like an Amsterdam diamond merchant. Amongst the group of wine collectors, journalists, and assorted "friends" who gather in his winery to taste his new Synergy wine, his moustache stands out. Synergy, a Cabernet Sauvignon/Merlot/Pinotage blend is not quite so hairy as its maker, but it does show his strength of character – a flinty integrity surrounding a big heart.

Distell

Distell is South Africa's largest wine company following the merger between Stellenbosch Farmers Winery and Distillers Corporation in 2001. Its current market capitalization is R2billion (US$200 million/ £114.4 million) and it boasts a forty per cent share of South Africa's premium-end wine market. It can manufacture and market 15 million cases of wine a year worldwide without breaking into a sweat. Distell runs wine farms in Stellenbosch, Simondium, Paarl, and Darling, with 1,518 hectares under vine. Linley Schultz is Distell's Australian winemaking chief and group general manager and at Nederburg in Paarl he presents a large array of wines.

Under the Nederburg label there is approachability. The Two Oceans range is for beginners. Obikwa, from the Adam Tas Cellars in Stellenbosch, is cheap and cheerful. The Oracle label is great fun and the Shiraz a breezy, brightly-berried, and bustling red. Oracle Sauvignon Blanc is an agreeable stainless steel-made artefact with dry lemon and slightly sour pineapple. The Hill & Dale label is "an unpretentious, accessibly styled brand made by international award-winning Stellenzicht winemaker Guy Webbe". The Chardonnay and Sauvignon Blanc are both charmingly unfussy. As is the Table Mountain range, a Chenin Blanc and a Merlot. The Tukulu label is marketed by Papkuilsfontein Vineyards, one of Distell's black empowerment ventures. The wines are made by Wellington Metshane, and his Pinotage knows how to throw its weight around. Neethlingshof Gewurztraminer is also emphatic and excellent with Chinese food. Drostdy Hof is the most impactful of Distell's brands. The Merlot has a fresh apple and plum finish with some alert berries and light tannins. The Pinotage has lovely chewy berries, plums, and finely roasted tannins as the wine cascades down the throat. The Cabernet Sauvignon thumbs its nose at clarets costing a whole bundle of notes more, offering as it does roasted berries, a hint of curry spice, and expansive tannins.

Rustenberg

This wine estate is managing directed with subtle flair by Simon Barlow, who took over from his dad. (Dad bought the farm in 1941, as relief from being an industrialist). Even in the pile of hay out in the paddock where calves chew the cud, there is a sense of design and purpose. As well as being a wine venture this is one of the oldest Jersey stud farms in the

153

country (the Barlows also also make their own cheese here). In 1987 it made just 6,000 cases of wine; it is now heading towards being a 100,000-cases-a-year winery (and introducing new grape varieties like Roussanne and screwcapping some of its wines). "We're not on the official Wynroute," says Simon proudly, "and we turn away coaches at the front gate. People find us. They know our wines."

As does Adi Badenhorst, the winemaker. If Rustenberg's wines betray the Barlow charm, they also reveal the Badenhorst style. Brampton Sauvignon Blanc is opulent and the Unoaked Chardonnay one of the most unpretentiously rich of its kind. Rustenberg Chardonnay is excitingly fruited and priced, combining creamy wood, melon/citrus fruit, and gunsmoke, and it has great elegance and charm. Five Soldiers Chardonnay is aromatic and complex.

Brampton Old Vines Red smells of apples (baked) which leads to seriously quaffable, correctly tannined red fruit. Brampton Cabernet/Merlot shows restrained plums and cherries.

Meerlust

Giorgio Dalla Cia has been making wine here in Stellenbosch since 1978, though the estate traces its history to 1693. Tradition dies hard here – unlike the wines, which die soft and succulent in the throat leaving, for the most part, very pleasant afterthoughts. As a conversational opening gambit between the sexes, "Meerlust darling?" is unbeatable: more provocative, surely, than anything Domaine de la Romanée Conti or Chateau Lafite has to offer as syallables on the tongue.

Lust indeed drives the estate: the lust to make wine like they used to make in Europe (in the good old days before the vineyards were sodden with chemicals and the peasants crushed the grapes with their calloused feet). Giorgio is a Friulian by birth, as stout as a rotunda, and with the solid stance of one of those old Roman gladiators – small in stature but as irresistible as granite (though Giorgio's grizzled white beard is more imperious, something you might find adorning the face of an Aurelian stoic). His wines are like he is: rounded, plump, sentimental, striving for completeness.

The Chardonnay he describes as being "Corton-Charlemagne in style". However, this is an insulting comparison if one moves forward from the peasants and considers the modern version of the legendary white burgundy. Giorgio's wine is creamy and smoky (the wood effect) and very finely structured. "At its best in seven or eight years from vintage," he suggests, but I would drink it within eighteen months.

The Pinot Noir offers baked plum, a touch of toffee, a slightly smoky undertone (again that wood!), and a perfume like Bresaola (the alpine cured beef). It is a polished and supple wine with a lingering fruitiness of great charm (Giorgio to a T). In spite of these virtues being obvious, its maker, quite madly in my view, says "it'll be at its peak at ten to twelve years of age."

De Toren
Emil den Dulk turns out De Toren Fusion V (Cabernets Sauvignon and Franc/Merlot/Petit Verdot/Malbec). It is richly clotted, about as subtle as an iron bar, and about as thick in the throat.

Waterford
This is an architectural chunk of the Tuscan seaside in view of the rocky outcrop known as the Helderberg (which reposes like the spinal column of some vast petrified dinosaur). The Waterford estate's Italian architectural heritage is obvious in its borrowings and the shadows it casts are Rococo. The wine is the same, the Cabernet Sauvignon being distinctly Tuscan and gently earthy in tone. Kevin Arnold, joint-proprietor, is another sentimentalist looking otherwards for inspiration. His Shiraz, which has some Mourvedre, is extremely meaty. Noted connoisseur Oprah Winfrey drank it at her fiftieth birthday party, it is said.

Rust-en-Vrede
This is a legendary estate run by Jean Engelbrecht, with Louis Strydom as its winemaker. Rust-en-Vrede is "rest and peace" in Afrikaans, or maybe "rest in peace", but the estate's Cabernet/Shiraz/Merlot is a magnificently combative wine of great resolve and character and the drinker cannot relax as s/he is carried away by its complex tributaries of fruit. The wine fully reflects both the repose of the estate and the Engelbrechts' aristocratic manner, along with the genteel paranoia of having to maintain a tradition stretching back to 1694.

De Trafford
David Trafford makes here several interesting wines (all showing the intensity of their maker), but the most unusual and stimulating is the "Vin de Paille". That is to say a sweet wine made from dried grapes (in Europe, dried on straw hence the name). The grapes are Chenin Blanc and so thick-knitted are they that the liquid could possibly defy consumption via a straw – a spoon might be more appropriate. Whatever, the result is a passionate wine, as madly delicious and wild as its maker, and the nuttily honeyed finish is a revelation.

Webersburg
Fred Weber and winemaker Rudi de Wet make something of a would-be Cabernet Sauvignon here. The wine can't quite make its mind up, but this is challenging to the drinker who likes a capricious liquid to study. Is it woody? Is it just juicy? Are there not some cunning tannins in there? This estate will get better and better.

Paradyskloof
Jan Coetzee, proprietor and winemaker here, greets the visitor dressed like Crocodile Dundee, but with legs like tree trunks, plus a handshake

which could turn the stopcock on a burst oil well. Yet his Vriesenhof Pinot Noir is like silk, all cosy elegance and finesse and it slips down like greased oysters. This ex-Springbok gives the appearance of massive indomitability, yet his wines tend towards softness and in some instances delicacy (the Talana Hill Chardonnay apart). He also loves wood. "I worked for some time in France. In the Forest," he says. "I try to marry the clone of the grape with the cooper." Thus he prefers Allier oak for Merlot, Nevers oak with Cabernets. He makes three ranges, Vriensenhof, Talana Hill, and Paradyskloof.

Laibach
Laibach's organic wine, The Ladybird (a Bordeaux blend), is outstanding. Its exemplary fruit shows calmness and softness, but it must be said this tasting was from the first vintage, from the barrel, and such a wine when bottled and aged will perform differently, with less passion. There needs to be a lot more organically farmed vineyards in the Cape.

Kanonkop
Johann Krige's normally delicious Kanonkop Paul Sauer Bordeaux blend was corked when, one time, he opened a bottle for me, and so he simply dashed off on his Harley-Davidson to get another from his vineyard cellar. If only all wine estates offered this service we restaurant diners would be much happier (though winemakers would be hugely the poorer and all those trips by motorbike would undoubtedly send them to early graves).

The answer, of course, is not two-wheeled transport but screwcaps.

Neil Ellis
This man is one of the pioneering spirits of the Cape wine industry, the first to set up a négociant type business in South Africa, sourcing grapes from relatively unknown regions such as Elgin and Groenekloof. Mr Ellis fills any room or landscape in which he is occupied – though he is not an especially large person (by the standards of a country which traditionally produces beefy stock), his persona is considerable; his determination like granite. He is immensely shrewd.

The spectacular views of the Jonkershoek foothills above the Oude Nektar estate (with its English public-park ornamental lake and swans) make a stunning backdrop for tasting the wines. Infinitely crunchier and sexier than its French prototype (Sancerre) is the Groenekloof Vineyard Sauvignon Blanc. The NE Coastal Shiraz has savoury tobacco and bitter cocoa. The Oude Nektar Shiraz is meaty. The NE Cabernet Sauvignon has tobacco and chocolate (so saving on the after-dinner mints and the cigar). The most dashing red, though, is the NE Vineyard Selection Cabernet Sauvignon. Its local Jonkershoek fruit, plainly showing its cold night-time locale, stiffens sinews, summons up the blood, and has heroic tannins.

Stellenbosch Vineyards

This is another major négociant, with a wide range of wines pitched (to hurl or throw with accuracy) at the global market. Chris Kelley, the winemaker, oversees the Cape Promise, Shamwari, Genesis, Kumkani, and Welmoed labels. Chris has a most original take on the screwcap versus cork debate (in which he, like most forward-thinking craftsmen, is on the side of the former). "I think very intensive cork taint is the winemaker's best friend," he says, startlingly. But think about it. He's right. In such circumstances the customer is much more able to understand, and far more quickly, why screwcaps are better. A thoroughly spoiled bottle of wine, tainted by its cork, which even a clod with a heavy cold could spot as faulty, converts people quicker than anything. The problem with cork taint, however, is that most of the time it is such a subtle thief that no-one notices it has made off with the fruit.

Meinert Wines

Martin Meinert is a very cautious individual hiding a heart of steel. "Is this the best harvest in thirty years in South Africa? That's what everyone tells me," I asked, regarding the 2003 vintage. Martin, who looks like a younger, less-barmy eyed version of Michael Douglas, purses his lips and strokes his chin and offers a ghost of a smile: "Maybe," he says. "But with only twenty-five per cent of the harvest in it's too early to say. I've seen wines change in tank and turn a harvest forecast on its head."

Swallowing these wise words, I proceed to swallow duck with polenta (with which the Meinert Cabernet Sauvignon was totally exquisite). It is a wine as polished as its maker, but to conclude the metaphor, at heart just as crunchy and considered, concentrated, and balanced. Martin understands texture. He suffers no fools, offers little surface ego, quietly takes the world in his stride yet, somehow, everything always comes out on his own terms. A good wine is like that. It makes you like it.

Thelema

Gyles Webb, if sent up from central casting for the part of a Cape winemaker, wouldn't even get past the doorman, let alone the film director. Gregory Peck's role in *To Kill a Mocking Bird*? Perfect. Cary Grant's in *North by Northwest*? Hmm. Maybe. As a result, the man's wines, bearing the Thelema label, show this slightly ironic, laidback charm, but reveal nothing of the immense energy and status of the man himself. Of the half-dozen individuals who can represent the South African wine industry on the world stage, Gyles makes a forceful case – not only because of his Cabernet Sauvignon, Merlot, Shiraz, Pinotage, Riesling, Chardonnay, and Sauvignon Blanc, but because of how beautifully the man's philosophical soul shines in those wines. He is also involved in the new Tolana range of wines, new on the market, but on first showing immensely impressive.

TOP Alicia, Malecka, and Erica (from left) grow up amongst the Springfield Estate's vines, where their father is an estate worker, and they have a huge playground.

BELOW LEFT A home-made water cooler and filter like this can only be found at Springfield. It would be a strong candidate, if entered, for the annual Turner Prize at London's Tate Modern art gallery.

BELOW RIGHT Danie and Lesca de Wet at De Wetshof, in Robertson, create famously consistent Chardonnays of great finesse.

Robertson
Land of warm, spicy thrills

I do not think there is another place on the vine trail of the Cape – the name of which promises so little yet delivers so much – as Robertson. The very name sends a cold flush of mistiness to enfold the spirit of the traveller who thinks, fondly perhaps, of the chilly vastnesses of the Highlands of Scotland. However, Robertson turns out to contain a lot of warm and spicy thrills, courtesy of the singular individuals who live and grow grapes there.

Graham Beck

Winemaker Pieter Ferreira has a touch of the swashbuckler and he lords it over an ultra-modern winery. Graham Beck vineyards is one of the neatest, tightest managed, most commercially astute yet quality driven operations of its kind in the Cape: 200 hectares of vines, 3,000 tons of grapes, 250,000 cases of wine; and able to go from the bottom end of the market to the top with ease and in style.

Graham Beck Brut non-vintage sparkling wine has crisp peach-strawberry subtleties and is very classy. The Blanc de Blancs 1997 gives Dom Pérignon and Krug a run for their considerable monies (for it has a luxuriously creamy edge which became even finer with age). The Graham Beck Pinot Noir/Chardonnay bubbly is intense, dry. The highly commercial Waterside White Chardonnay/Colombard shows touches of dry peach and Ogen melon to charming elegance of citricity. Railroad Red Shiraz/Cabernet is quaffably easy going with its plum/cherry fruit. The Graham Beck Pinno Pinotage shows good tannins to its generally roustabout fruit. Graham Beck Merlot is juicily plummy. BG Shiraz has classy tannins coating smoky fruit. Graham Beck Cabernet has biscuity tannins. Old Road Pinotage is vibrant with life, tannins, and spicy fruit. The Ridge Syrah shows lingering chocolate fruit. Graham Beck Cape Blend, a marriage of forty per cent Cabernet Sauvignon, thirty per cent Pinotage, and thirty per cent Cabernet Franc, is world class in texture and weight, presenting the palate with gorgeous tannins and cocoa-drenched dry fruit. Cornerstone Cabernet has lovely rich tannins and chocolate and prune fruit.

Pieter is a foodie who loves cooking (and these things are made evident when one is merely tasting with a winemaker because the passion for food translates itself into the wines). "You can divorce a lot of things in life," he tells me, as if I needed any telling, "but you can't divorce wine and food."

De Wetshof Estate

The de Wets have the distinction of having set up the first registered winery in Robertson and were the first to appreciate the area's rich high-ph limestone soil (with matching perfect viticultural climate). Danie is one of the largest figures (physically, commercially, and

intellectually) in the Cape wine industry, his wife one of the shrewdest and most dynamic of women. Not only does Danie have this, his own business, but he is also chairman of the KWV – the Ko-operative Wijnbouwers Vereiniging. The KWV, which started as a co-operative movement designed to give members control of the market rather than merchants, became a bureaucratic monster (referred to by producers when its officials visited and laid down the law as the KGB). Nowadays it looks outwards, exporting five million cases of wine, and getting involved in black empowerment schemes.

On nearly 162 hectares of vines, Danie, who learned winemaking at the Geisenheim wine university on the Rhine, has made his name with Chardonnay. But there is some Riesling and, lately, Pinot Noir too.

The man puts his huge, yet delicate, personality into all his wines, but especially the Chardonnays. Danie de Wet Sur Lie Chardonnay is simply the most elegant Chardonnay for the money on sale in the UK. De Wetshof Finesse Chardonnay is more complex, chalky with a floral undertone. African Eagle Chardonnay displays demure melon and citrus. De Wetshof d'Honneur Chardonnay offers slightly smoky charentais melon fruit with cream. De Wetshof Single Vineyard Bateleur Chardonnay has a soft vegetal richness like some magnificent quirky Meursault.

Springfield Estate
Here I am talking to the ex-dentist whilst her rugby-loathing brother potters in the cellar. Can this be South Africa? The weather is like the Luberon (Provence) in late May (or October). Neither Jeanette Bruwer (who no longer asks anyone to open wide except when pouring her wine) or Abrie Bruwer look South African, but their wines are – indelibly.

A glass of Springfield Sauvignon Blanc washes the day's cares away and restores hope to this representative of the cynical species. Indeed, it adds inspiration to the normal cutting gooseberry fruit, for Springfield is one of the most serious yet happiest wine estates in the Cape. It is possible to be committed yet not fanatical, detached yet not insular, wild without being whacky, and humane without being sentimental – and the remarkable Springfield estate proves it.

Life From Stone Sauvignon Blanc is stunningly classy and chewy with fine minerals and gooseberry. Special Cuvée Sauvignon Blanc invokes a large sigh and the reflection, "Sancerre growers, eat your hearts out!" The wine has a certain tropicality, but is hugely elegant overall. Wild Yeast Chardonnay is a magnificently textured, complex, satiny white wine showing no wood and no-nonsense deliciousness. "Ach, the longevity of wild yeast wines!" exclaims Abrie.

The estate's red wines show different sides of their maker's philosophical personality. The Blend "Under The Impression" is forty per cent Merlot, forty per cent Cabernet Franc, and twenty per cent Cabernet Sauvignon and 100 per cent original. It is savoury with an undertone of coffee. Wholeberry Cabernet Sauvignon has dainty tannins, a hint of jam, and touch of chocolate on the finish. The Work of Time is a red blend offering intense leathery fruit, spice, and long tannins huddled together splendidly texturally.

Springfield Estate also has another label called Firefinch. Firefinch Sauvignon Blanc is concentrated pure gooseberry with a lime under- tone. Firefinch Colombard/Chardonnay is a "nice summer wine" according to its maker, but this damns it with faint praise for it has lovely refreshing peach/lemon fruit. Firefinch Ripe Red "What The Birds Left" is a *mélange* of fifty per cent Merlot, thirty per cent Ruby Cabernet, and twenty per cent Cabernet Sauvignon which manages to be jammily ripe yet dry, finishing off with a touch of spice. The Single Vineyard Cabernet is pure chocolate.

Elim
As new as new can be
It is, I would guess, fairly boring growing wheat and raising sheep or tending apple orchards. Growing grapes to make wine is far sexier. And a lot more profitable. The area of the Cape known as Elim is not one to yet include in the league of great New World wine regions like McLaren Vale, Franschhoek, or Napa, for it is so new that when local wheat farmers and sheep herders first conceived the ambition that perhaps wine grapes might grow succulent and disease-free on their land, warm and windy during the day as it was, dry and cold at night thanks to the proximity of the most southerly point of Africa, Cape Agulhas, the wine bureaucrats at KWV told them to get stuffed. Such was the power of the KWV in those days that that was the end of the dream, but today Elim has got people like Francis Pratt growing wine grapes and Bruce Jack to do the winemaking. Bruce, from his Flagstone winery in Somerset West (qv), is a tireless ambassador for the Cape, with his own often spectacularly individual wines. He and Francis Pratt have the Berrio range as a joint venture.

Before I depart, Francis shows me around his cellar. It is full from floor to ceiling with barrels, perhaps as many as four. "Welcome to the smallest and most southerly wine cellar in South Africa," he says.

LEFT One hears a lot about marine influences on wines, and how beneficial it is for vineyards to enjoy a littoral climate. However, Abrie and Jeanette Bruwer of Springfield took this to a new level (six fathoms, to be precise). The Bruwers dumped some of their top wine, Methode Ancienne Cabernet Sauvignon 1997, with the corks covered in wax, in the Atlantic off the Cape in March 2000. It was fished up on New Year's Eve 2003. A bottle was given to me and on Valentine's Day 2004 I opened it, even though two of my dinner guests owned property in Bordeaux and are wedded to that region's Cabernets. The bottle was opened, its contents poured into a jug and when, an hour later, the jug stood empty, along with everyone's glasses, I was forced to confess that my wine racks could yield nothing comparable to follow. James, one of the two Bordeaux lovers, wistfully remarked, "Not unless you've got the 1982 Chateau Lafite."

RIGHT Wine from Elim is yet to make an international name for itself, but give it time and more producers like Francis Pratt, and wines like the ones here, and the area will surely become renowned.

Walker Bay (Hermanus, Hemel-en-Aarde Valley)
Elegant, polished, very well mannered

Peter Finlayson appears and greets the visitor with the measured aplomb, deportment, and head of the Duke of Kent. The Bouchard Finlayson estate, as it curves down the Hemel-en-Aarde Valley, is equally stately to regard through the tasting room's mullioned windows.

Surprisingly, it is a recent phenomenon, being established only in 1989. The Bouchard element has, though, gone (though contact is maintained, so it was said, with Paul Bouchard in Burgundy). The Tollman family trust is the main shareholder, Mr Finlayson being joint managing director and winemaker/vineyard manager. Peter Finlayson is committed and dedicated, but his wines are more loquacious and elegantly intrusive (as it should be – winemakers who speak louder than their wines generally turn out superficial liquids).

The Blanc de Mer, a vigorous Riesling/Kerner/Gewurztraminer/ Chardonnay/Pinot Blanc assembly, is haughty and not one whit as soppy as the blend of grapes might suggest. The Sauvignon Blanc 2002 is classic. Chardonnay Sans Barrique dry and peachy. Crocodile's Lair Chardonnay is courageously creamy yet crisp with great character and staying power. Mission Vale Chardonnay is so svelte and finely tailored it makes most white burgundies seem like rags. On the red side Hannibal, a remarkable Sangiovese/Pinot Noir/Mourvedre/Nebbiolo/Barbera blend, is a firm hedgerow-fruity, quaffing wine. Far grander are the finely made Pinots Noirs, Galpin Peak Tete de Cuvée with its classic bouquet of gamey strawberry and Galpin Peak with its hint of liquorice. This estate is like a far-flung branch of a Savile Row tailor – the address is different, but the cut is unmistakably, immaculately Old World. The spitting image of Finlayson himself.

Hamilton Russell

Anthony Hamilton Russell's dad was an ad man; he ran J Walter Thompson SA for years, and like so many men whose routine but well paid jobs give them time to reflect and fall in love with wine, he wanted to reproduce the great burgundies he enjoyed. So he planted Chardonnay and Pinot Noir, just as they do in Burgundy, and then proceeded to make the nattiest wines of their kind in the Cape. The estate ran into difficulties after a while and Tony bought it from his dad, who's now retired.

The Hamilton Russell wines? Copies of burgundies *bien sur*. That's what dad aimed at, that's the tradition the son carries on. But not copies of modern burgundies. It is important to grasp the distinction here. Modern burgundies – the Pinot Noirs – contain a lot of arrogant rubbish (the exceptions are known and glorious). It's old style burgundy that's worth copying: the stuff that spills over with provocative, truffle-scented smells and flavours with that shockingly feral, louche-yet-luxurious undertone which suggests Bacchanalia on forest floors.

The Pinot Noir here is, then, especially shocking. Decanted wholly for five hours before drinking, and served chilled, it requires serving in a goldfish bowl of a glass with goat's cheese on Poilane toast with fresh black truffle shavings. The estate encourages this sort of decadence.

Beaumont

This estate is in Bot River, within the Walker Bay enclave, and it is well worth visiting. Jane Beaumont is as jolly as a headmistress at end of term time and the winery has a nicely low key charm (as likely to offer for sale a relative's home-made jewellery as the wine). The last winemaker here, Niels Verburg, who has been replaced by Wilhelm Kritzinger, was an impressively solid individual who given a black suit and tie would pass for one of the more terrifying bouncers to be seen outside New York night clubs.

Interestingly, all the tasting bottles Mr Verburg showed me had been opened for twenty-four hours. But there was something even odder about the wines inside. Each had a saline, Islay malt whisky tang, first wine to last: Chenins, Chardonnays, Pinotages, and red blends. The most insistently delicious wine was the Pinotage. It oozed flavour as if it had been squeezed from a tube. It had spice as well, and that salty tang was not as intrusive as it was with the other wines. I asked Niels about the distinctive tang. "It's all the sweat which goes into making the wines," he said with a grin. "We do get a sea breeze every afternoon, though."

Mr Kritzinger, perhaps a less salty character, will presumably create a different take on the fruit which comes from the Beaumont vines.

Newton Johnson

If the home designed by Felicity Newton and built by husband Dave Johnson, 400 metres (1,312 feet) above sea-level in the hills above the Walker Bay, were a winery open to the public, it would be a major tourist attraction. It is isolated, alone amongst the mature fynbos, handsomely and polychromatically in bloom, and outside the door hyrax haggle, miniature tortoises tread, blue-headed lizards lounge, duikers dash, klipspringers kringe, jackal buzzards blow, rock kestrels roam, baboons babble, grysboks gambol, leopards leap, porcupines prickle, cobras collect, and honey badgers beat – though they do all of these things at a discrete distance from the house so they are invisible to the visiting wine taster who is not distracted. Dave Johnson, though, swears they're there, in the surrounding hills, playing hard to spot.

Newton Johnson wines also offer interesting views; short range, with the outrageously commercial export First Cape label, to long range with wines like the exquisite NJ Chardonnay from Kaaimansgat (Crocodile's Lair) vineyards at Villiersdorp – luxurious, creamy, and woody, but very elegant – as well as a Cabernet Sauvignon, a Pinot Noir, and a Shiraz/Mourvedre. The upper range wines show deftness with power and I would anticipate their getting sassier every vintage.

LEFT One of the Cape's newest and most beguilingly crisp Sauvignon Blancs overshadows a model of the estate's homestead.

RIGHT Cape Point Sauvignon Blanc: on a vine post is another worthy newcomer to the burgeoning South African wine scene.

Elgin

From apples into grapes. A growing reputation for great fruit

Andrew Gunn not only grows patently thrilling grapes to make Iona Sauvignon Blanc into a deliciously modern artefact, he runs his estate on modern principles. The workers are shareholders.

The vineyards are situated high on the ridges above Elgin, on the ocean side of the valley. The land was once occupied by apples destined for UK grocers. The Sauvignon Blanc is a limpidly thrilling wine with its crunchy gooseberry fruit and crisp, complex acids. Andrew Gunn's principles are superbly rewarding to mull over, to tease the palate with, to swallow.

Paul Cluver Estate

Thandi is a profit-sharing farming venture in Elgin between the state, local community workers, and private enterprise – the first of its kind in South Africa. The project was initiated by Dr Paul Cluver and he's put some real money behind it. He is a remarkable individual. Few men can walk long distances with one hand in their pocket and the other over their hearts.

The wines here are a Sauvignon Blanc, a Chardonnay, a Riesling, a Pinot Noir, and a Cabernet Sauvignon. No wine is opulent, being dry and restrained (one Late Harvest 2001 aside, which will be amazing in 2008 when it's ready to astonish) – they do have something quiet and determined to say, but will never express it in wine competitions.

Dr Paul Cluver, a neuro-surgeon, is a tall figure with the steady dignity and pale, interiorized features of a monastery archivist. He is like his wines, without one whit of the usual male ego. About the black empowerment scheme he has initiated, the so-called Thandi project, he is fluent. The project owns 200 hectares, with around ninety under fruit and thirty-five or so under vine.

"The idea started in 1995. With a redundant forestry industry. I said why don't we take the land and give the people working there a share of

it? Fruit and forestry to begin with, then vineyards in 1996. We saw the greatest opportunity in wine for the project because with wine you make a premium product. You can't add much value to fruit, but you can with grapes. The main shareholders became the workers. The first year we made a profit was 2003."

Thandi

Susan Kraucamp, whose husband Patrick makes Thandi wines and works in the winery, is wearing a summery dress and a summery smile. As she talks, I taste.

Thandi Chardonnay has good firm, melon fruit, as good as anything from the New World in its price range. The Pinot Noir is creamy and soft. I wish, in fact, there were not so much emphasis on Pinot Noir in South Africa (much better would be Pinot Gris).

"I was a secretary," says Susan: "My husband was a fork lift truck driver. We went to the Cape Wine Academy. My husband went to Portland Oregon and became a winemaker and now he makes the wines for Thandi. These wines."

Somerset West

Haute couture grapes

Vergelegen is an historic estate which dates back to 1700. In some respects, it occupies the same place in the imagination of the locals as does Hampton Court in Londoners' minds and Versailles in Parisians'.

André van Rensburg makes the wines here and he is the nearest thing to a one-man band in this wine country. If each grape variety is an instrument, he plays it as well as it can be played – with precision and feeling, unerringly conscious of its potential.

Vergelegen Sauvignon Blanc Reserve is one of the most potent in the Cape, offering pineapple, grapefruit, and lemongrass. Vergelegen Chardonnay Reserve has an elegant woodiness, rich citrus and melon tones: "It needs a serious amount of time in bottle," says André. A three year-old example, from a good vintage, appears: it is a nigh-perfect specimen (19 points out of 20? Possibly).

Vergelegen White (thirty per cent Sauvignon Blanc, seventy per cent Semillon, percentages will vary with each vintage) can be like a rich Graves but with more silky fruit and an ineffable and exciting, exotic undertone. The same wine, different vintage, comprised seventy-eight per cent Sauvignon Blanc and twenty-two per cent Semillon and it was herbaceous and bitter-lemony: "Ten years easy," says André, referring to its longevity. "Maybe," I retort, but not with a cork in its neck, only if it has a screwcap will it develop into something in ten years.

Vergelegen Shiraz is gorgeous, opulent and ripe with hints of tobacco and catering chocolate coating sturdy tannins. Vergelegen Merlot has intense coffee-fruit, quite remarkably delicious, with sensationally sensual tannins. Open this wine five hours before drinking and decant.

Vergelegen Cabernet Sauvignon (with maybe fifteen per cent Merlot) has a raw cocoa powder richness and needs to mature two or three years from vintage before it really purrs. Vergelegen Cabernet Franc/Merlot flaunts tannins, liquorice, coffee, chocolate, nuts, earth, and herbs, and has a luxurious texture (silky – almost a touch slinky). Vergelegen Red (a Cabernet Sauvignon/Merlot/Cabernet Franc blend) shows complex world-class fruit – chocolate, coffee, cocoa, and touch of sweet berried richness as the tannins caress the back of the throat. And then lastly there is "V", just "V", a Cabernet Sauvignon/Merlot marriage of intensity and passion of which only 600 cases have been made. No fining, no filtration, this is Andre's personality in a liquid. "I call it FL," he says: "my F**k Lafite wine."

I have never tasted a Lafite as solid, or as sensually perfumed, as André's "V" – and that includes the 1933, 1937, 1945, 1947, and 1949 vintages, all drunk in the 1960s with the exception of the 1933 which I drank in 1983. Though the 1976 tasted in barrel with Lafite's cellar master had a fine texture when tasted in 1978, André's "V" outclasses it. It is a perfect Cabernet/Merlot blend of bewitching cocoa, chocolate, spice, tannin, and satin textured richness overlaid with corduroy and hints of dry herb. It is an utterly bewildering wine of crunch yet caressing fruit – that ultimate paradox of great wine with its superb balance. It melts in the mouth and lingers for minutes.

Flagstone

Bruce Jack is eloquent and excitable, as easy to talk to (and as quick to see all the possibilities in a phrase or gesture) as a politician seeking urgent re-election. Only Charles Back carries more impact in his words, more meaning in his measured expressions, and greater wealth of ideas in his head. Mr Jack, of Scottish stock originally, has a canny mind of which he makes full use. He exudes the red-cheeked authority of a scouts master, confident his words carry weight. I sit there drinking his Flagstone Music Room Cabernet Sauvignon and think myself well entertained indeed.

"The best way to enjoy this wine," he assures me, "is to put it into a decanter, put it into the microwave for twenty-five seconds, and then into the fridge for twenty minutes, then back into the microwave for twenty-five seconds. It ages five years in that time and becomes perfect drinking. It softens everything. Gets rid of the volatiles."

He has many original ideas about wine.

"You can change a wine by playing loud music at it. The chemistry is electromagnetic. It's the same thing with pumps in the winery. Not good. The use of pumps changes the hydrogen/oxygen balance, plus and minus. Gravity is the best way to handle wine during the vintage."

I take these thoughts home to bed with me. Led Zeppelin at Pinotage perhaps? Palestrina at Chenin Blanc? Imagine the effect of Emma Kirkby on Cabernet Franc.

TOP Dave Newton and wife Felicity, of Newton Johnson estate, drink to the setting sun.

CENTRE Kathy and Gary Jordan of Jordan Wines make accessible yet very provocative liquids.

BELOW Charles Back of Fairview Estate with grower Christo Briers-Couw at the latter's Eenzaamheid Farm (which proudly has 1693 carved over the farmstead door). They are tasting Shiraz from Christo's Solitude vineyard which Charles rates exceptionally highly.

Paarl
Ten thousand years of history

Capitalist, conjurer, philanthropist, punster, agricultural aristocrat, and all-round marketing and winemaking genius. That is the protean Charles Back of Fairview Estate. Charles is a visionary but no dreamer. He makes his dreams, and the dreams of others, concrete.

Fairview Estate itself comprises some 273 hectares of land of which around 176 are vines. There are also 600 goats and several buildings including two schools, workers housing (set around a pleasant green square), and the cheese factory (Africa's most productive). There's even a surgery for the resident nurse/medical officer.

"I'm a capitalist," says Charles Back: "But one with a very strong social conscience. If you lack that you destroy the things which make you viable as a business."

We stop off at Eenzaamheid Farm (1693 over the farmstead door) so we can taste the fruit at grower Christo Briers-Couw's Solitude vineyard which Charles rates highly for its Shiraz grapes.

"We always pay more for our grapes," says Charles. "Then we get our viticulturalist to move in. Then we address ourselves to labour issues." He smiles. "We've got the best paid people around."

And some of the tastiest Shiraz grapes in the Cape on the evidence of the ones Christo grows. "We pick on phenolic ripeness," says Charles, "not sugar". That is to say that it isn't the ripeness of the fruit inside the berry which is so important as the ripeness of the tannins in the skins. When later in the cellar I tasted a barrel sample of the same Solitude Shiraz, I rated it 19 points out of 20 for it is a remarkable wine showing a grilled tomato aroma, big tannins of grip yet civilized demeanour, a liquorice undertone, and scrumptious chocolate fruit. The finish, so beautifully thick and textured, leaves the taster with the impression of having crunched mocha coffee beans (medium roast). Nothing exemplifies the proposition of this book – that individuals make wine not vineyards – more potently than Charles Back. His personality is evident in each and every wine he produces, whether the wine costs £5 or £15, whether the wine is made from Pinotage or Chardonnay, whether the wine is from his own vines or those under contract. His are always elevated wines, whatever the elevation of the vineyard.

Another Fairview brand is Spice Route, one of the most impressive range of Cape wines on sale in the UK. When winemaker Charl du Plessis demonstrates how carefully the basket press squeezes the grapes and how meticulously the band of women on the sorting table select the grapes, it is easy to understand why.

"I pay them 350 Rand (£33) a week during the harvest season to sort grapes," explains Charles. "It's about what a male truck driver gets. Some of the co-ops here should employ people like that. We have this huge untapped labour force. Who needs machinery when we have so many people wanting to work?"

Fair Valley and the great insight

There are several black empowerment schemes in the Cape other than Fair Valley (another Charles Back initiative). This new project involves sixteen hectares of vines, eight houses, a cellar, and a tasting room on the way. However, 1998 was the first vintage in South Africa to bear the fruits of a black empowerment scheme. The Skipper's brothers' wine it was and it was called New Beginnings. New Beginnings Classic Dry White 1998 and New Beginnings Classic Dry Red 1998 were both made by Mattheus Thabo at the vineyard and he owed his chance to make wine under such historic conditions to the far-sightedness and wisdom of Alan Nelson of the Nelson wine estate in Paarl. It was he who gave ten hectares of vineyard land, in 1997, to the sixteen families who worked his vines and it was he who encouraged Mattheus Thabo to train and become a winemaker.

The greatest wine revolution possible in the Cape has yet to materialize, however. This revolution would see vast numbers of black South Africans regularly sitting down to dinner with a Cape Cabernet Sauvignon on the table and not bottles of beer or some other beverage.

I ask Awie Adolf, Fair Valley's winemaker, about this. We're sitting by the fountain in the garden outside the Fairview winery shop (a shop which true to the Back tradition of commercial nous is packed with visitors, hordes of them carrying wine and cheeses to their cars). Awie purses his lips and his cheeks are sucked in. It's a lean face radiating an

RIGHT Awie Adolf, Fair Valley's winemaker, contemplates his life's work and, perhaps, his children's futures.

intense sense of the big man within rather than the slight man without. He's looking at this own red wine in a big glass as he speaks, regarding it with detachment as if searching for a fault which might transmit itself to the interviewer's eye.

"I was not a wine drinker. From time to time maybe. But I'm not a person who drinks wine every day – even now."

"It's a wonderful project for me. We have got our own house. First time, my friends were sceptical. When I got involved. Now they see our house. They see the difference."

For a second, as he sighs, I think he's going to remove the cap and wipe his forehead. But he smiles a bare smile: "If I die, there's a house for my children. No-one can tell me to leave my house. No-one can tell my children to leave their house."

So this is the great insight. This was what made Mr Adolf's remarks the most original of any Cape winemaker's. He was doing what he did not for himself. He was doing it for his children. For his wife and family. For the first time, perhaps for the first time ever, certainly for the first time in generations of Adolfs, he was a property owner.

Landskroon

Paul De Villiers makes wines here with decidedly delicate personalities. A Chardonnay, Cabernet Sauvignon, and Shiraz all show a level of suavity and couthness which to some people may seem atypical, but to this observer provide yet more evidence that subtle yet determined winemakers make subtle yet determined wines. There is a show of Bushmen artefacts at this estate, which have turned up during vineyard digging over the years. It was Charles Back who first took me to see the collection and he passed an immortal remark as we studied a flint axe-head 10,000 years old. "Bang go all those fables," said Charles, "about there being nobody here before the Dutch settlers arrived."

Mont Destin

Mont Destin. My destiny. Here's a typical piece of male sentimentality for you. This vineyard and guest house is on a hill and it's Ernst and Samantha Burgin's place – Ernst being a German who had an olive farm in Provence until Samantha, a visitor from the Cape, happened to breeze by and that was that. Next thing you know the olive farm's sold and Sam has lured Ernie, as he's now called, to the Cape and they've set up a vineyard and a nice home with the traditional thatched roof, and over the winery there are guest rooms. The usual dogs lumber about or lie around, though one novelty not seen elsewhere is a pair of miniature, camera-shy, Vietnamese-style black pigs who enjoy poking their snouts into any edible-looking junk on the ground from a clump of weeds to a camera bag (minus cameras). The wines here are impressive, in particular the alcoholically intimidating Bushvine Pinotage which is absolutely terrific with a spicy casserole.

TOP A goat that is not roaming around the Fairview Estate in Paarl. But it is, at times, free to do so along with 600 of its kind kept here. Hence this estate's legitimate use of the Goats do Roam label which has so infuriated the French.

BELOW LEFT The pupils at Fairview Estate's infants school confront their first British wine writer and find something to smile about.

BELOW RIGHT The removal of the marc, or pomace, which is left behind after the juice has been run off is an essential task at all wineries. This winery is the Fairview Estate's.

RIGHT-HAND PAGE

TOP The Cape can boast some of the most original vineyard backdrops in the world. Here, Paarl vines flourish by the early-evening, pinkly-suffused granitic presence of the Simonsberg.

CENTRE LEFT Pre-dinner apéritifs at Mont Destin with local winemakers (including Monty Waldin, British writer on organic wines): Peter de Wet of Excelsior; Bertus Fourie and David Sonnenberg of Diemersfontein; Bernhard Veller of Nitida; Jose Condé of Condé Stark; Alastair Rimmer and Corrine Smit of Aguste; Dudley Wilson and Wittem Roussow of Terra Organica; Samantha and Ernst Burgin of Mon Destin.

CENTRE RIGHT Charl du Plessis has made the Spice Route wine range into one of the Cape's most spectacular successes with critic and wine drinker alike.

BELOW A 1957 Studebaker Champion on sale by the side of the road for 30,000 Rand (£2,800) excluding would-be chauffeur.

Coleraine Wines

Clive Kerr at this estate makes a rich and couth Coleraine Culraithin Shiraz. It has yet to be exported.

Warwick Estate

The Chardonnay here has been one of the most consistently impressive, priced as it has been in the UK at under £10 a bottle, for some years. Whatever the vintage, it was invariably capable of maturing well for a couple of years and achieving a creamy vegetality of the kind the most ardent Chardonnay grower would swap his grandmother for. But Mike Ratcliff, managing director, can also show his visitor some classy reds: a Cabernet Franc; a Cabernet Sauvignon; a Pinotage; and, most compelling of all, Trilogy (a blend of the two Cabernets and Merlot) which has richly balsamic tannins. It also has a Cape Blend.

What is a Cape Blend? It is a wine which meets the criteria set down by officialdom. A Cape Blend cannot be a blend of any grapes to which the maker takes a fancy. A Cape Blend can only be a wine with no less than thirty per cent, no more than seventy per cent, of the local grape, Pinotage. I have experienced Beyers Truter's Synergy (from Beyerskloof), Warwick Three Cape Ladies, Clos Malverne, Dellrust, Kanonkop, Flagstone, Simonsig, Grangehurst's Nikela, Kaapzicht, and Onyx Kroon Groenekloof. The two most dramatic on recent showings were Clos Malverne Auret Reserve and Flagstone Dragon Tree Reserve.

Les Garagistes – or rather The Car Porters?

The term *les garagistes* was originally coined some years back to cover an emerging group of young Turks in Bordeaux who more or less made wine in their garages – they had little do do with the established wineries or châteaux. The group of Cape winemakers who have arrogated the term have convened at the home of Clive Torr, in Topaz Street, Somerset West, whose car port now serves as his winery and his back garden as his vineyard.

Mr Torr amazed his neighbours by planting 411 Pinot Noir vines instead of lawn. The vineyard takes up the whole of the garden which is in a tightly packed suburb of detached homes.

"The motley crew," as he calls his fellow *garagistes* as he introduces them to me and, one by one, they parade their wines. From a neighbouring house down the hill, towards the ocean (which can be glimpsed), a burst of repulsive rock music breaks out. "Someone's son," grimaces Clive.

The first of the wines, a William Everson Chardonnay, is poured out and the alfresco tasting commences. Then it is the turn of Topaz Pinot Noir, then Scali Pinotage, then Anthill Pinotage, Anthony Smook Cabernet Sauvignon, and then wines from Lance Nash (Black Pearl Wines), Akkerdal, and Blyde. The Topaz Pinot Noir is quietly – well, not so quietly in actual fact – stunning.

Wellington, Durbanville, and Franschhoek
Diemersfontein

Bertus Fourie and David Sonnenberg of this estate shared with me a bottle of their Diemersfontein Carpe Diem Pinotage 2001 which, although very slightly tainted by its cork, was still drinkable, though it was like hearing a Schubert sonata, D894 perhaps, with the thumb of the pianist's right hand missing. One's enjoyment, though marred, was not entirely ruined (bit like a scratched record I suppose). One could appreciate the chocolate richness of the fruit and recognize that, in perfect condition, the wine would rate 18 points out of 20 (priced under ten quid a bottle).

Bellingham

Lunch with winemaker Graham Weerts (who's since gone to Kendall-Jackson in California) was a treat at this historic estate, founded in 1693, as it was impossible to drink little of a magnificent barrel sample of Merlot. I'd rate it 17 points out of 20 if he would promise to keep the tannins in it and not egg-white-fine them out. Graham has been replaced by Niel Groenenwalk who's come over from Pederberg.

Mischa Estate

Andrew Barns produces here a ripe monster of a Cabernet Sauvignon which nicely clogs the throat.

Nitida

Bernhard Veller's Cabernet Sauvignon is a big wine, intense, rich, but not neurotic. His Pinotage can be even more alcoholic, around 15% ABV.

Boekenhoutskloof

Marc Kent looks like a Greenwich Village hippy circa 1969 and he is just about as laid back. Marc is the man behind Porcupine Ridge and The Wolf Trap Red, two brilliant labels deservedly selling many thousands of cases to Britain.

The Wolf Trap (a Cabernet Sauvignon/Syrah/Cinsault/Pinotage blend) is a wonderfully warm wine with touches of liquorice and leather and gripping yet succulent tannins. Porcupine Ridge Merlot has berried-up-to-its-neck fruit which smells of barbecued herby sausages with thyme. Porcupine Ridge Cabernet Sauvignon is soft and chocolate-drenched. Porcupine Ridge Syrah fills the senses with ripened riches, balanced wood, and a classy finish.

Mark's estate wines are even more arousing. Boekenhoutskloof Semillon is overwhelming, with an aroma of lanolin, a hint of frustrated honey. The texture is waxy, vegetal and dry, with bitter yet untwisted fruit; a delicious, elegant finish. Boekenhoutskloof Syrah is extravagant, highly polished, sveltely tannic. Boekenhoutskloof Cabernet Sauvignon gives you coffee with dry tannins.

TOP LEFT A pair of incisive white wines from one of the Cape's most dynamic producers.

TOP RIGHT The Cape's single most famous wine: Vin de Constance from Klein Constantia estate.

BELOW LEFT Vanie Padayachee, sous-chef of Le Quartier Français, a guest house restaurant of sublime excellence in Franschhoek. Vanie cooked me a lunch with Boekenhoutskloof wines which included the most exquisite chicken liver paté in the world.

BELOW RIGHT (From left) Achim von Arnim of Cabriere Estate, Gotfried Mocke of Chamonix, and Nigel McNaught of Stoney Brook wonder if it's time for another game of *boule*.

Cabriere Estate

No-one in the Cape makes wines like Achim von Arnim. He is an outpost of resilient conservatism in a sea of post-modernism. Cabriere Tranquille is a sweet apéritif wine. Haute-Cabriere Chardonnay/Pinot Noir Sparkling is plump. Haute-Cabriere Pinot Noir is like a jam-filled biscuit. In conversation, Achim von Arnim spends most of the time talking about Burgundy and not once does this charming and amusing man mention the Cape and the glory of its vineyards. "We're not New World," he insists, and he is right. He is not New World. Cabriere's wines are Old World from cork to punt, nose to throat.

Constantia
English butlers and Napoleon

Buitenverwachting is one of those curses of a word isn't it? It has certainly lived up to being "beyond expectations". For it was beyond expectations in reality for years as owner after owner (some sixteen, I believe, before the present German couple, the Muellers, acquired it) came and went and failed to make it pay. But now it is one of the most beautifully restored wineries, homes, places for visitors to eat and picnic, and indeed place to work (immaculate conditions for the workers), in the Cape as a whole and in Constantia, where it is situated, in particular. One finds here a lovely Chardonnay, deftly wooded and wittily fruity, which manages to be both a first-class food wine as well as something sufficiently provocative to toy with in a glass by itself.

Constatia Uitsig

Lunch here is by way of the La Colombe restaurant where the food is edible and advanced in technique. The wines of Constantia Uitsig are not quite so advanced and not nearly so edible. They are led by a gripping Sauvignon Blanc but there are also a Cabernet/Merlot, a Chardonnay Reserve, and a haughty Semillon Reserve.

Klein Constantia

This is a historic estate established in the seventeenth century by the Dutch governor of the Cape, Simon van der Stel. The estate's legendary Vin de Constance is a sweet dessert-style wine, which though intensely sweet can lack botrytis complexity (from nobly rotted grapes). It needs at least fifteen years to become really interesting. It is claimed that Napoleon became partial to it in exile, discovering it in all probability via his English butler on St Helena. For years the wine was barred EU entry, but it has now been reprieved. It was a victim of the French inspired plot to keep non-EU sweet wines out of Europe via a dastardly and preposterous plan that any wine of non-EU origin which contained residual sugar sufficient to carry it into a different tax bracket if the wine was re-fermented could not be imported. Vin de Constance has recently been allowed back into the EU and thus the UK. Tasting the 1997 Vin de Constance in 2003 in the Cape with a local wine celebrity he passed the remark that "it's a pity they can't make wines at Klein Constantia as well as they describe them". I couldn't possibly comment but I do wonder if that remark would have been passed if the vintage had been, say, 1947?

LEFT-HAND PAGE

TOP Andre van Rensburg, winemaker, greets newly arrived grapes at Vergelegen.

CENTRE LEFT Lucy Warner, exporter, and Ken Forrester, producer, make a swinging couple.

CENTRE RIGHT Children of a fisherman at Arniston Bay keen to sell a painted ostrich egg and miniature seascape for 50 Rand (£4.70).

BELOW Neil Ellis has profound views on wine and he can also offer spectacular views of his vineyards.

RIGHT-HAND PAGE

TOP The old-world elegance of Anthony Hamilton Russell's home overlooks his new world vines.

BELOW LEFT Marc Kent of Boekenhoutskloof Estate makes the Porcupine Ridge and Wolftrap wine ranges, as well as superb top-end Cabernet Sauvignon and Syrah and a magnificent Semillon.

BELOW RIGHT Peter Finlayson of Bouchard Finlayson carries himself with a dignified almost ducal reserve and his subtle yet powerful wines reflect this imperiousness.

South Africa's winemakers

STELLENBOSCH

BEYERSKLOOF
PO Box 107 Koelenhof 7605
Tel: 21 865 2135. Fax: 21 865 2683
wine@beyerskloof.co.za
Winemakers: Beyers Truter, Anri Truter

DE TOREN PRIVATE CELLAR
PO Box 48 Vlottenburg 7604
Tel: 21 881 3119. Fax: 21 881 3335
info@de-toren.com
www.de-toren.com
Winemaker: Emil and Sonnette den Dulk

DE TRAFFORD WINES
PO Box 495 Stellenbosch 7599
Tel/Fax: 21 880 1611
info@detrafford.co.za
www.detrafford.co.za
Winemaker: David Trafford

DISTELL
PO Box 184 Stellenbosch 7599
Tel: 21 809 7000. Fax: 21 886 4611
info@distell.co.za
www.distell.co.za
Winemaker: Linley Schultz

DORNIER WINES
PO Box 7518 Stellenbosch 7599
Tel: 21 880 0557. Fax: 21 880 1499
info@dornierwines.co.za
www.dornierwines.co.za
Winemaker: Ian Naude

KANONKOP ESTATE
PO Box 19 Elsenburg 7607
Tel: 21 884 4656. Fax: 21 884 4719
wine@kanonkop.co.za
www.kanonkop.co.za
Winemaker: Abrie Beeslaar

KEN FORRESTER
PO Box 1253 Stellenbosch 7599
Tel: 21 855 2374. Fax: 21 855 2373
ken@kenforresterwines.com
www.kenforresterwines.com
Winemaker: Ken Forrester, Martin Meinert

LAIBACH VINEYARDS
PO Box 7109 Stellenbosch 7599
Tel: 21 884 4511. Fax: 21 884 4848
info@laibach.co.za
www.laibach.co.za
Winemakers: Stefan Dorst, Francois
van chase

JORDAN WINERY
PO Box 12592 Die Boord 7613
Tel: 21 881 3441. Fax: 21 881 3426
info@jordanwines.com
www.jordanwines.com
Winemaker: Gary Jordan

MEERLUST ESTATE
PO Box 15 Faure 7131
Tel: 21 843 3587. Fax: 21 843 3274
info@meerlust.co.za
www.meerlust.co.za
Winemaker: Giorgio Dalla Cia

MEINERT WINES
PO Box 7221 Stellenbosch 7599
Tel: 21 865 2363. Fax: 21 865 2414
info@meinertwines.com
www.meinert.co.za
Winemaker: Martin Meinert

NEIL ELLIS WINES
PO Box 917 Stellenbosch 7599
Tel: 21 887 0649. Fax: 21 887 0647
info@neilellis.com
www.neilellis.com
Winemaker: Neil Ellis

PARADYSKLOOF
PO Box 155 Stellenosch 7599
Tel: 21 880 0284
info@paradys.co.za
www.paradys.co.za
Winemaker: Jan Coetzee, Richard Philips

RUSTENBERG WINES
PO Box 33 Stellenbosch 7599
Tel: 21 809 1200. Fax: 21 809 1219
wine@rustenberg.co.za
www.rustenberg.co.za
Winemakers: Simon Barlow, Adi
Badenhorst

RUST-EN-VREDE
PO Box 473 Stellenbosch 7599
Tel: 21 881 3881. Fax: 21 881 3000
info@rustenvrede.com
www.rustenvrede.com
Winemakers: Louis Strydom, Ettienne
Malan

STELLENBOSCH VINEYARDS
PO Box 465 Stellenbosch 7599
Tel: 21 881 3870. Fax: 21 881 3102
info@stellvine.co.za
www.stellvine.co.za
Winemakers: Chris Kelly, Carmen
Stephens, Morne van Rooyen, Pieter
Kleinhans, Danie van Tonder, Albert
Basson, Anthony Meduna

THELEMA
PO Box 2234 Stellenbosch 7601
Tel: 21 885 1924. Fax: 21 885 1800
wines@thelema.co.za
www.thelema.co.za
Winemakers: Gyles Webb, Rudi Schultz

WATERFORD
PO Box 635 Stellenbosch 7599
Tel: 21 880 0496. Fax: 21 880 1007
info@waterfordestate.co.za
www.waterfordestate.co.za
Winemakers: Kevin Arnold, Francois
Haasbroek

WEBERSBURG WINES
PO Box 3428 Somerset West 7129
Tel: 21 851 7417
weber@iafrica.com
www.webersburg.co.za
Winemakers: Rudi de Wet, Giorgio Dalla
Calla (advisor)

ROBERTSON
DE WETSHOF ESTATE
PO Box 31 Robertson 6705
Tel: 23 615 1853
info@dewetshof.com
www.dewetshof.com
Winemaker: Danie de Wet

GRAHAM BECK WINES
PO Box 134 Franschhoek 7690
Tel: 21 874 1258. Fax: 21 874 1712
market@grahambeckwines.co.za
www.grahambeckwines.co.za
Winemaker: Jaques Conradie

KRANSKOP
PO Box 18 Klaasvoogds 6707
Tel/Fax: 23 626 3200
kranskop@myisp.co.za
www.kranskopwines.co.za
Winemaker: Nakkie Smit

SPRINGFIELD ESTATE
PO Box 770 Robertson 6705
Tel: 23 626 3661. Fax: 23 626 3664
info@springfieldestate.com
www.springfieldestate.com
Winemakers: Abrie Bruwer, Johan van Zyl

WALKER BAY
BEAUMONT WINES
PO Box 3 Bot River 7185
Tel: 28 284 9194 Fax: 28 284 9733
beauwine@nelactive.co.za
www.beaumont.co.za
Winemaker: Sebastian Beaumont

BOUCHARD FINLAYSON
PO Box 303 Hermanus 7200
Tel: 28 312 3515. Fax: 28 312 2317
info@bouchardfinlayson.co.za
www.bouchardfinlayson.co.za
Winemaker: Peter Finlayson

HAMILTON RUSSELL
PO Box 158 Hermanus 7200
Tel: 28 312 3595
hrv@hermanus.co.za
Winemaker: Hannes Storm

NEWTON JOHNSON
PO Box 225 Hermanus 7200
Tel: 28 312 3862. Fax: 28 312 3867
wine@newtonjohnson.com
www.newtonjohnson.com
Winemaker: Gordon Newton Johnson

ELGIN
IONA VINEYARDS
PO Box 527 Grabouw 7160
Tel: 28 284 9678. Fax: 28 284 9078
gunn@iona.co.za
www.iona.co.za
Winemaker: Andrew Gunn

PAUL CLUVER ESTATE
PO Box 48 Grabouw 7160
Tel: 21 844 0605. Fax: 21 844 0150
info@cluver.co.za
www.cluver.com
Winemaker: Andries Burger

THANDI WINES
PO Box 12730 Die Boord
Stellenbosch 7613
Tel: 21 886 6589
rydal@thandi.com
www.thandi.com
Winemaker: Patrick Kraukamp

SOMERSET WEST
FLAGSTONE WINERY
PO Box 3636 Somerset West 7129
Tel: 21 852 5052. Fax: 21 852 5085
admin@flagstonewinery.co.za
sales@flagstonewinery.co.za
www.flagstonewines.com
Winemakers: Bruce Jack, Wilhelm
Coetzee, Marlize Beyers, Elize Wessels,
Gerald Kakijana

TOPAZ WINE
26 Topaz Str Heldervue, Somerset West
7130. Tel: 21 855 4275
topazwines@mweb.co.za
Winemakers: Clive Torr and Tanja Beutler

VERGELEGEN
PO Box 17 Somerset West 7129.
Tel: 21 847 1334. Fax: 21 847 1608
vergelegen@amfarms.co.za
www.vergelegen.co.az
Winemaker: Andre van Rensburg

PAARL
AKKERDAL ESTATE
PO Box 36 La Motte 7691
Tel: 1 876 3481. Fax: 21 876 3189
wine@akkerdal.co.za
www.akkerdal.co.za
Owner/winemaker: Pieter Hanekom

ANTHILL WINES
14 Somerset Street, Somerset West 7130
Tel: 21 855 4275. Fax: 21 855 5086
anthill@absamail.co.za
Winemaker: Mark Howell

BLACK PEARL WINES
PO Box 609 Suider-Paarl 7624
Tel: 83 297 9796. Fax: 21 863 2900
lancelotnash@absamail.co.za
www.blackpearlwines.com
Winemaker: Lance Nash & family

BLYDE
PO Box 3231 Paarl 7620
Tel: 83 270 5706. Fax: 21 872 8799
lieb@blyde.com. www.blyde.com
Owner/winemaker: Lieb Loots

CLOS MALVERNE
PO Box 187 Stellenbosch 7599
Tel: 21 865 2022. Fax: 21 865 2518
closma@mweb.co.za
www.closmalverne.co.za
Winemaker: Isak Smit

COLERAINE WINES
PO Box 579 Suider-Paarl 7624
Tel: 21 863 3443. Fax: 86 617 8723
info@coleraine.co.za
www.coleraine.co.za
Winemaker: Clive Kerr

DELLRUST WINES
PO Box 5666 Helderberg 7135
Tel: 21 842 2752. Fax: 21 842 2456
dellrust@mweb.co.za
www.dellrust.co.za
Winemakers: Albert Bredell, Arno Cloete

FAIR VALLEY WORKERS ASSOCIATION
PO Box 583 Suider-Paarl 7624
Tel: 21 863 2450
marlene@fairview.co.za
Winemaker: Awie Adolph

FAIRVIEW
PO Box 583 Suider-Paarl 7624
Tel: 21 863 2450. Fax: 21 863 2591
info@fairview.co.za
www.fairview.co.za
Winemakers: Charles Back, Anthony de Jager

KAAPZICHT ESTATE
PO Box 35 Koelenhof 7606
Tel: 21 906 1620. Fax: 21 906 1622
kaapzicht@mweb.co.za
www.kaapzicht.co.za
Winemakers: Danie Steytler, with Charl Coetzee

GRANGEHURST WINERY
PO Box 206 Stellenbosch 7599
Tel: 21 855 3625. Fax: 21 855 2143
winery@grangehurst.co.za
www.grangehurst.co.za
Winemaker: Jeremy Walker

KANONKOP ESTATE
PO Box 19 Elsenburg 7607
Tel: 21 884 4656. Fax: 21 884 4719
wine@kanonkop.co.za
www.kanonkop.co.za
Winemaker: Abrie Beeslaar

LANDSKROON WINES
PO Box 519 Suider-Paarl 7624
Tel: 21 863 1039. Fax: 21 863 2810
landskroon@mweb.co.za
www.landskroonwines.com
Winemakers: Paul de Villiers, Fanie Geyser

MONT DESTIN
Wine Farm and Guest House. PO Box 1237, Stellenbosch 7599
Tel/Fax: 21 875 5040
wine@montdestin.co.za
www.montdestin.co.za
Winemakers: Samantha Burgin, Bruwer Raats

SCALI
PO Box 7143 Noorder-Paarl 7623
Tel: 21 869 8340. Fax: 21 896 8383
info@scali.co.za
www.scali.co.za
Winemakers: Willi & Tania de Waal

SIMONSIG FAMILY VINEYARDS
PO Box 6 Koelenhof 7605
Tel: 21 888 4900. Fax; 21 888 4944
wine@simonsig.co.za
www.simonsig.co.za
Winemakers: Johan Malan, Van Zyl du Toit, Debbie Burden

SMOOK WINES
PO Box 7038 Noorder-Paarl 7623
Tel: 21 872 1804. Fax: 21 872 2867
asmook@mweb.co.za
www.cheninblanc.co.za
Winemakers: Anthony Smook, with Francois Louw

WARWICK ESTATE
PO Box 2 Elsenburg 7607
Tel: 21 884 4410
info@warwickwine.co.za
www.warwickwine.co.za
Winemaker: Louis Nel

WILLIAM EVERSON WINES
7 Prospect Street, Somerset West 7130
Tel: 82 554 6357. Fax: 21 851 2205
we@intekom.co.za
Winemaker: William Everson

WELLINGTON
DIEMERSFONTEIN WINES
PO Box 41 Wellington 7654
Tel: 21 864 5050
wine@diemersfontein.co.za
www.diemersfontein.co.za
Winemakers: Bertus Fourie, Francois Roode

BELLINGHAM
PO Box 79 Groot Drakenstein 7680
Iel: 21 874 1011
bellingham@dgb.co.za
www.bellingham.co.za
Winemakers: Niel Groenewald, Lizelle
Gerber, Mario Damon

MISCHA ESTATE
PO Box 163 Wellington 7654
Tel: 21 864 1019/20. Fax: 21 864 2312
mischaestate@telkomsa.net
www.mischa.co.za
Winemaker: Andrew Barns

DURBANVILLE
NITIDA ESTATE
PO Box 1423 Durbanville 7551
Tel: 21 976 1467. Fax: 21 976 5631
nitida@mweb.co.za
www.nitida.co.za
Winemakers: Bernhard Veller, Jacus Marais

FRANSCHHOEK
BOEKENHOUTSKLOOF
PO Box 433 Franschoek 7690
Tel: 21 876 3320. Fax: 21 876 3793
boeken@mweb.co.za
Winemakers: Marc Kent, Rudiger
Gretschel, Heinrich Tait

CABRIERE ESTATE
PO Box 245 Franschoek 7690
Tel: 21 876 2630. Fax: 21 876 3390
cabriere@iafrica.com
www.cabriere.co.za
Winemaker: Achim von Armin

CONSTANTIA
BUITENVERWACHTING
PO Box 281 Constantia 7848
Tel: 21 794 5190. Fax: 21 794 1351
info@buitenverwachting.com
www.buitenverwachting.com
Winemaker: Hermann Kirschbaum

CONSTANTIA UITSIG
PO Box 402 Constantia 7848
Tel: 21 794 1810. Fax: 21 794 1812
wine@icon.co.za
www.uitsig.co.za
Wine Director: Andre Badenhorst

KLEIN CONSTANTIA ESTATE
PO Box 375 Constantia 7848
Tel: 21 794 5188. Fax: 21 794 2464
info@kleinconstantia.com
www.kleinconstantia.com
Winemakers: Adam Mason, Trizanne
Pansegrouw, Corina du Toit

Garagistes
ONYX KROON GROENEKLOOF
PO Box 114, Darling, 7345
Tel: 22 492 2276
Fax: 22 492 2647
infu@darlingcellars.co.za
www.darlingcellars.co.za
Winemaker: Abe Beukes

Index

Pages with winemakers'
addresses are shown in **bold**;
italic page numbers indicate
illustrations.